D0726450

P eyond the Bea........

WITHDRAWN FROM
THE LIBRARY
UNIVERSITY OF
WINCHESTER

KA 0202357 1

Beyond the Beanstalk

Interdisciplinary Learning Through Storytelling

Lynn Rubright

UNIVERSITY OF WINCHESTER
LIBRARY

Heinemann
Portsmouth, NH

· **Heinemann**
A division of Reed Elsevier Inc.
361 Hanover Street
Portsmouth, NH 03801–3912
Offices and agents throughout the world

© 1996 by Lynn Rubright

All rights reserved. No part of this book may be reproduced in any form or by electronic or mechanical means, including information storage and retrieval systems, without permission in writing from the publisher, except by a reviewer, who may quote brief passages in a review.

Acquisitions Editor: Lisa A. Barnett
Production Editor: Renée M. Nicholls
Cover Designer: Linda Knowles
Manufacturing Coordinator: Elizabeth Valway
Author photo by Monty Levy

The author and publisher wish to thank those who have generously given permission to reprint borrowed material:

Grim and Gloomy by James Reeves. © James Reeves from *Complete Poems for Children* (Heinemann UK). Reprinted by permission of the James Reeves Estate.

Library of Congress Cataloging-in-Publication Data
Rubright, Lynn.
    Beyond the beanstalk: interdisciplinary learning through storytelling /
Lynn Rubright.
        p.   cm.
    Includes bibliographical references (p.   ).
    ISBN 0–435–07028–2 (alk. paper)
    1. Storytelling.   2. Interdisciplinary approach in education.
I. Title.
LB1042.R83   1996
372.64'2—dc20   96–9057
                                                                    CIP

Printed in the United States of America on acid-free paper

Docutech RRD 2006

To my husband, Robert Rubright,
and our sons,
Ted and Dan,
To my parents, Martha and Ed Laue,
without all of whom this book would not
have been written

Contents

Foreword   xi

Preface   xiii

Acknowledgments   xv

Introduction   xvii
     Project TELL   xviii

1   Beyond the Beanstalk: An Interdisciplinary
     Storytelling Unit   1
       Jack and the Beanstalk: Learning the Story's Bones   1
       Initiating Project TELL With "Jack and the
         Beanstalk"   2
       Story Weaving   3
       The Writing-Reading Connection   6
       Jack Tale Story Quilts: Art/Language Arts Extension   7
       Drama, Math, Social Studies   7
       Language Arts   11
       Storytelling Across the Curriculum   12

2   Frog and Toad's Garden: Storytelling, Drama,
     Science, Poetry   13
       The Garden   14
       From Story to Poetry Writing   17

3   *Rosie's Walk*: An Interdisciplinary Approach   23
       Rosie's Walk "Teaches" Reading   23
       Large Group Story Weaving   25
       Rosie's Walk: Connections to Interdisciplinary Studies   29

4   Bellerophon and Pegasus: Storytelling and Movement   33
       Bellerophon and Pegasus: A Synopsis   34

5	The Sea: Movement, Stories, and Poetry	37
	Plate Dance (Large group exercise)	38
	Space Walk (Large group exercise)	38
	Underwater Walk (Large group exercise)	39
	Mirror Game (Working in pairs)	39
	Poetry Writing (Large group session)	41
6	Storytelling and Music	45
	Carl Orff Methodology	45
	Arnold Lobel's "The Camel Dances"	46
	Creating a Sound Story	48
7	Children as Playmakers and Playwrights	51
	Improvisational Playmaking	51
8	Learning Tales to Tell—Quick and Easy: Listening and Reading	61
	Quick and Easy Method to Learn a Tale to Tell from Text	62
	A Teacher Tells "The Sun and the Wind"	65
	The Power of Storytelling to Reach, Touch, and Teach	67
	The Copyright Issue	69
9	Ananse the Spider: Storytelling African Style	71
	Multicultural Storytelling: Ananse's Dance	71
	Ananse the Spider Storytelling Unit	74
10	Family Folklore: Storytelling and Creative Writing	75
	Elders Share Their Stories	76
	"Baked Potatoes"	77
	Creative Writing: Children's Family Stories	81
	Alice Jackson's Classroom Visit	83
	Alice Stories	85
11	History Telling: An Oral History Project	89
	Meramec Highlands	89
	Final Product: The Kirkwood Book	91
	The Writing Process: A Reflection	93
12	Eldertel: Senior Citizens and Children Share Stories	95
	Making Connections Through Song and Dance	95
	Group Puppetry	96

13 Storytelling and the Writing-Reading Process: An Interview
    with June Von Weise   99
        The Writing Process   99
        Literature Response Journals   103
        Literature Circles   104
        Using Multicultural Literature   105
        Poetry   107
        The Author Cycle   107

14 Artist-in-Residence Programs   109
        Metro Theater Circus (MTC)   109
        Two Residency Programs   111

15 Stories to Tell—Quick and Easy   115
        Jack and the Beanstalk   115
        Bellerophon and Pegasus: A Greek Myth   119
        Aesop's Fables—Retold by Lynn Rubright   120
        Ananse the Spider Tales—Retold by Lynn Rubright   131
        The Man Who Tried to Change His Luck:
            A Traditional Tale, Adapted by Lynn Rubright   137

Appendix A: Then and Now: A Family Folklore Interdisciplinary
            Storytelling Unit   141
        Language Arts Activities in the Family Folklore Unit 141
        Social Studies in the Family Unit   141
        Math and Sciences   142
        Art   142
        Music   142
        Festival of Family Folklore: Finale   143
        Getting Started   143

Appendix B: Storytelling, Movement, and Drama Exercises   147
        Movement Vocabulary   147
        Ways to Move   147
        Storytelling, Movement, Drama Exercises   148

Appendix C: Bookmaking
        Materials   159
        Directions   159

Glossary   163

Bibliography   167

Foreword

"Is it ready yet?" I could taste that cake as I stood waiting by the oven. "Not yet," my grandmother would answer, as she had just answered five minutes before. "Good things take time." How I looked forward to those good things from the oven, and how I have looked forward to this book by Lynn Rubright. Six years in the writing, it has been thirty years in the making. How glad I am to see it emerge from the oven. My copy will soon be devoured—dog-eared, notes in the margins, highlights throughout. Not the sort of academic prose destined to gather dust, unopened on the shelf, this book will quickly become a mainstay of my work.

I count myself among the thousands who have been transformed by Lynn Rubright's teaching. It was Syd Lieberman, an award-winning educator, author, and master storyteller himself, who first said to me, "Nobody teaches teachers like Lynn Rubright; she's my mentor." At his urging, I invited her to create a course at Northwestern University. That was over a decade ago; Lynn has taught for us many times since that first, magical summer.

To see Lynn Rubright teach—well, this part is hard to describe. It's a little like seeing a jazz musician at work. She is a master of improvisation. She has made play a vital component of her life's work. Her words dance. Her rhythms are syncopated. She sings, whispers, dances, cries, exalts, laughs out loud in unexpected places—her classroom is a place of discovery, of celebration, of growth. She reminds me that once all teachers were performing artists. And yet she is quick to yield center stage; her artistry lies in her ability to empower her students. Soon they are doing things they never dreamed of doing; her students, many of them teachers, find the safety and inspiration in her classroom to take extraordinary leaps of faith. A transformation occurs.

Experiencing her exercises for the first time, I urged Lynn to compile them into a book. Nobody was doing what she was doing. She was teaching whole language long before anybody knew what to call it. She teaches integrated arts because she doesn't see them as the least bit isolated from one another. Multicultural? Of course. It is part and parcel of the world of the folktale. Crosscurricular? Well certainly. Each discipline informs the other. Once there was a time when all teachers were storytellers; Lynn Rubright takes us forward to a place we have known before—a place where a story, in all its richness, is at the heart of a larger learning experience.

"Now is it ready?" The chime had rung but still we waited. "Yes," she said at last, "It's ready." Good things take time. For storytellers everywhere, for teachers, for teachers of teachers—I am so glad *Beyond the Beanstalk* is out of the oven. There will be plenty to share. Let the feast begin.

Rives B. Collins
Associate Professor of Theatre
Northwestern University

Preface

By their nature, the arts are experiential, engaging, and involving. More classroom teachers are discovering what arts specialists have always known: that storytelling, drama, movement, music, and other experiences in the expressive and visual arts can:

- release tension and relax children
- promote inventive thinking and problem-solving skills
- expand the imagination
- broaden one's knowledge base
- encourage spontaneity
- generate innovative, creative responses
- provide environments for different learning styles
- stimulate interactive and cooperative learning
- increase self-esteem and self-confidence
- enhance self-expression
- develop understanding and appreciation of aesthetic principles
- nurture listening skills, increasing concentration and ability to recall information
- bring content areas to life
- create interdisciplinary bridges
- modify negative behavior patterns
- provide opportunities to explore diverse cultural heritages
- be a springboard into reading and writing activities

When the arts are integrated across the curriculum, content becomes meaningful to children, and learning takes place.

Beyond the Beanstalk shares with teachers tried-and-true ways to use the many dimensions of storytelling and other expressive arts in their classrooms, both as skills they might develop for themselves to enhance their teaching styles, and as a motivational teaching tool.

It is hoped that teachers who explore the many applications of storytelling, in particular, will encourage their students to become storytellers, too.

Acknowledgments

This book could not have been written without the support of many people. William Freeman introduced me to the joy of dance and movement. Zaro Weil deepened my appreciation and understanding of the importance of arts in education. Jim and Carole Maronek offered me a cottage in the north woods where I could work in peace, summer after summer. They also provided expert advice on creative drama. My husband, Robert Rubright, helped me revise and revise. Master teachers June Von Weise, Belinda Wilucki, Amy Beabout, Barbara Tuley, Leslie Handley, Martha Jander, Sue Hinkel, Pat Vogl, Kate Kollman, Vera Karsch, Sandra Miller, John Rusyniak, and Marie Theerman taught me more about thematic, interdisciplinary approaches to curriculum design.

Dr. Gail Huffman-Joley emphasized how children must connect experiences with meaning before learning takes place. Dr. Marlene Birkman and Dr. Paul Steinmann encouraged me never to stop growing. Dr. Fred Stopsky said, "Don't give up." Dr. Bill Lyons confirmed my belief in the importance of storytelling and its connections between listening, imagining, and reading and writing processes. Dr. Ben Halm helped me understand the importance of multiculturalism in the classroom. Ted and Dan Rubright, my sons, inspired me when they were young and became my mentors and teachers as they grew up. Dr. Thomas Keating saw possibilities for using the arts in education; he suggested we design Project TELL. Constance Levy demonstrated the power of poetry in the lives of children. Syd Lieberman, Rives Collins, Mary Stigall, Ruthilde Kronberg, Emily Thach, and Annette Harrison showed me new ways to use story and drama, and how it is possible to be performance artist, writer, and teacher. Marilyn Probe helped me see how elders and children can interact through the arts. Dr. Andrea Rothbart confirmed my belief that mathematics are integral to the arts. Diane Dino gave invaluable technical assistance.

Principals Lawrence Combs, Pam Stanfield, Max Loudenslager, and Leslie Palmer opened their elementary schools to me and my university students as we endeavored to help children learn, using the arts across the curriculum. My grandmothers told me stories, and my parents, Martha and Ed Laue, honored my need for time and space to think, work, and play. Bill Martin, Jr. said "Write it down!" And I did.

Introduction

This book demonstrates how broadly storytelling can be defined and interpreted and how useful it is as both art form and teaching tool. Readers will learn about the power and potential of stories and how to become effective storytellers who can employ movement, drama, music, creative writing, poetry, and, most vitally, improvisational play.

Beyond the Beanstalk should be especially helpful for:

- teachers and their students
- librarians
- educators who train in-service and future teachers
- school district administrators and board members
- parents
- professional storytellers and other artists such as poets, dancers, musicians, mimes, and drama specialists who seek to contract with school districts to present their services

Years ago, Dr. Thomas Keating, the new superintendent of our school district, asked me to suggest an alternative way to teach reading. I was the district's resident storyteller and fine arts consultant, following years as an elementary classroom teacher and performer with a touring children's theater company. I strongly suggested storytelling as a key alternative method to approach the teaching of writing and reading. Storytelling, I advised, is more than merely learning something to tell—a folk, fairy, or literary tale; a myth or legend; or a historical or personal anecdote. Storytelling encompasses the bulk of our communications with others. Stories can form the basis of many things we study or experience to enrich and enliven our curricula.

What empowers teaching with stories? When a story is well told, we listen in a special way, entering the story ourselves. Our imaginations are fired up. We connect psychologically, emotionally, intellectually. We are there. Stories transmit information to children without their having to read the text. Having listened to a story, students are frequently motivated to read the tale. Children who are poor readers are often willing to tackle the text of a story with understanding after they have heard a story told. When teachers tell stories in the classroom, they discover that their students are often motivated to read more about a subject and then write and tell their own stories about the topic in their own creative ways.

"Apply for a federal grant that focuses on how storytelling and other arts can serve as pivotal approaches to teach reading and writing" the superintendent instructed. And so I did.

PROJECT TELL

Our grantsmanship yielded a three-year nonrenewable Title IV-C government grant. We named it Project TELL—Teaching English Through Living Language. Although the new program was designed mainly for third graders and, less intensely, for eighth-grade drama students in our suburban St. Louis school district, teachers of other grade levels were invited to participate if they wished. The grant stipulated that the teacher training sessions be open to the public. We beamed newspaper advertising to teachers from private schools and other districts in the community, announcing workshop dates and storytelling topics. Interested local residents were also welcome. Soon parents, grandparents, clergy, and Sunday School teachers were regularly attending our sessions; a few health care professionals interested in the power of storytelling in the healing process also attended. Throughout the three-year life of the program, classroom teachers and district and university reading specialists helped us shape storytelling activities to use as tools to assess increases in student reading comprehension and writing skills. When district teachers, including some from the local high school, realized that the stories and extension activities initially targeted for third and eighth graders worked— with some minor adjustments—with students at *all* grade levels, they joined the ranks of the Project TELL "storytelling teachers."

One Project TELL objective called for participating students to broaden their understanding of six components of story plot (story bones): setting, character, incident, crisis, conflict, and resolution. Another objective aimed to help students develop storytelling skills that included improvisation and creative drama. Eye contact, voice, facial expression, and gestures were honed to establish character, set mood, and create special effects. Eighth-grade drama students prepared stories to tell to younger students, who reversed roles and told them to eighth graders. Storytelling tours and festivals for both grade levels became major program components throughout the district.

Participating teachers and others who attended from the community at large were urged to discover and then develop their own storytelling skills, mostly through coaching and practical experience at the monthly teacher training workshops. Movement, creative drama, and pantomime were staple activities since they were key factors in rendering stories and had potential for involving students in integrated language arts exercises that could bridge curricular content areas.

Initially, not everyone was enthusiastic about Project TELL. One school board member called it "another example of the misuse of federal funds." Later, when parents told him how their children were telling *Beowulf* and Norse myths at home and reading complex renderings of the tales, he became a convert. He referred to Project TELL as the "new reading program."

Over the years I have had opportunities to both train and work with teachers throughout the United States and abroad who wish to become more effective storytellers and to use the art in their classrooms. Those who use it consistently report how storytelling has changed their teaching styles. Most readily agree that:

- Effective teachers are often natural storytellers.
- Opportunities to use storytelling can arise anytime during a class period, regardless of subject area.
- Stories in all guises fill people's lives—as personal experiences, family lore, gossip, lunchroom conversation, as well as specifically researched, carefully crafted pieces that fill special curricular needs.
- Storytelling undergirds basic communication skills: listening, speaking, writing, and, consequently, reading, and can enhance comprehension of difficult content material.
- Storytelling assists both interactive and collaborative learning in the classroom.
- The more teachers and their students open themselves to playful experimentation with stories, the more possibilities there are for varieties of renderings to unfold.
- Through storytelling workshops, teachers recognize and experience their own potential as skilled storytellers, and by modeling

storytelling in their classrooms, they enable their students to become more effective storytellers, too.

- Storytelling, combined with dramatic play, allows children to try on many roles, helping them develop the ability to empathize, increasing understanding of those different from themselves.
- Teachers are often surprised at the insights children reveal as they ponder the complex meanings of fables, folktales, and other literature they have heard or read.
- When children tell stories they often reveal gifts and talents that have gone undiscovered with traditional approaches to learning.
- Storytelling offers many children an opportunity to develop skills and excel in oral expression, gaining respect that they had not experienced before from peers.

Of course, most teachers are still obligated to cover and follow prescribed, mandated material. But with inventive thinking, playfulness, and a willingness to grow, explore, and risk, teachers repeatedly report that there is wide latitude for creativity when they use storytelling and other expressive arts as a way to enrich and enliven their existing curriculum. Teachers who have ventured forth to explore teaching possibilities that include storytelling in its many venues discover that their students don't wait for the 3 P.M. bell to ring so "real life" can resume. They have discovered that storytelling is often the key to engaging students in "real life" all day long.

1

Beyond the Beanstalk
An Interdisciplinary Storytelling Unit

Adaptable Through Grade Six

When I was four years old, one of my grandmothers came to our two-flat in Chicago to nurse my mother and tend my newborn sister. My other grandmother, who lived upstairs, took care of me.

Nestled together under the covers of the feather bed for our midday nap, Grandma Pickett told me stories before we fell asleep. Again and again I begged her to tell "Jack and the Beanstalk." "But, Lynnie, I told you 'Jack' yesterday." "I don't care, Grandma, tell it again." When she dozed, I'd jab her. "Wake up, Grandma. Tell me what happens next!"

"You know what happens next, Lynnie, why don't you tell it?"

"No, Grandma, you tell it!"

Years later, I realized that my own love of stories originated with my grandmother's fairy tales. I wondered if I could learn to tell Jack to my own young sons in the way my grandmother had told the tale to me. Reading the story several times to mentally establish the setting, characters, sequence of events (incidents), and ending, I practiced telling "Jack" over and over in my own natural language. Mine was a simple learning technique, which I referred to as "learning the story's bones"—through visualization, and definitely *not* through word-for-word memorization.

JACK AND THE BEANSTALK: LEARNING THE STORY'S BONES

Visualize the setting: Jack's thatch roof cottage where he lived with his destitute and irritable mother.

1

Visualize the characters: a scrawny Jack; his grumpy mother; old Milky White the cow, skinny and dry as a bone; the Little Man who coaxed Jack to swap the cow for five magic beans; the giant's wife; the giant with his sack of gold; the hen that laid golden eggs; and the singing harp.

Visualize the sequence of events (incidents): Jack's mother insisting he sell the cow for a good price; the Little Man tricking him into trading her for beans; the three trips up the beanstalk and the return home with the treasure: gold, hen, and harp. The pursuit of the furious giant who fell and killed himself as Jack chopped down the beanstalk.

Visualize: Jack and his mother live happily ever after, maybe.

After I told "Jack" to my sons in this way, they insisted, "Tell it again, Mommy." Sprawled over sofa cushions on the floor, they listened intently as I told it again. And again.

In ensuing weeks they acted "Jack" out during their play. From the kitchen I'd hear laughter. Peeking into the living room I found Ted pretending to chop down the beanstalk in pantomime, while Danny, in pajamas stuffed with pillows, bumped and rolled down the carpeted spiral staircase, plopping onto the living room floor, pretending to be the dead giant. Jumping up, Danny declared, "Now it's my turn to chop down the beanstalk."

One day, I tripped over a puppetlike figure Danny had created by spreading pieces of clothing—boots, hats, scarves, jackets, pants—on the floor. "Mommy, you messed up my giant," he complained. We put his giant, including oranges for eyes and a banana for a mouth, back in place.

INITIATING PROJECT TELL WITH "JACK AND THE BEANSTALK"

Early in Project TELL, I decided to tell "Jack" in the third-grade classes; the teachers proposed interdisciplinary follow-up activities to extend "Jack" with their students. *Initially, my telling "Jack" was meant to model storytelling to help the teachers and their students see ways in which they themselves might employ storytelling.* Soon we came to see how telling "Jack and the Beanstalk" had become the springboard for connecting curriculum areas in many surprising ways. Science, social science, and math seemed to grow naturally from the story, with teachers often following the interests of their students.

Improvisational movement and drama games helped children explore issues concerning interpersonal relations as part of social studies. Creating sequels to "Jack and the Beanstalk" by playing an interactive storweaving game called Whatever Happened to Milky White? led to creative writing and reading connections. These stories became know as Jack tales.

STORY WEAVING

Whatever Happened to Milky White?

After the characters and objects from "Jack" are listed on the board, the children agree on something around which to spin a new Jack Tale.

Jack
Jack's Mother
Milky White, the cow
Little Man
Giant
gold
hen
harp
five beans
Giant's Wife
dead Giant's body

Students then choose one item from the board. Next, a story weaver (a person in the class, or the teacher) asks questions to generate information. The story weaver blends this new information into the unfolding tale. This game can be played with the whole class, with one story weaver, or in small groups, each with a designated story weaver. Sometimes the new "Jack Tale" evolves informally with everyone working collaboratively, taking turns as story weaver. Some children, catching on to the idea of making sequels, prefer making up and sharing their own individual Jack Tales.

Story Weaving a New Jack Tale: An Example of the Process

Mary, one of Marie Theerman's third-grade students, had heard me tell "Jack and the Beanstalk" earlier in the day. Now, she came to class from her remedial reading session as I was explaining story weaving. "About whom or what shall we make our new Jack Tale?" Mary waved her hand excitedly. "I want to know about Princess Marie," she said.

Her classmates stared at her. I glanced at Mrs. Theerman, who shrugged. No Princess Marie appeared on the board.

I asked Mary, "Who is Princess Marie?"

"Princess Marie is the girl who married Jack," said Mary.

This kind of response happens to me often. Right after explaining directions, someone contributes an idea that fits nothing we have talked about. As story weaver, I have to make a decision. I can say, "But there wasn't a Princess Marie in the story—please choose a person or object listed on the board." Or I can accept the fresh idea by announcing, "Okay, this Jack Tale is going to be about how Jack got married to Princess Marie." Which I did.

"Yay," yelled a delighted Mary.

The secret to successful story weaving is keeping the class focused and occupied by continually asking them questions, weaving each new segment into the developing plot. Of course, the story weaver has no idea how the story will turn out in this highly improvisational process. As we begin Mrs. Theerman takes notes on the unfolding story.

"Everybody knew Jack married Princess Marie, but few knew much about her or how their marriage came to be. Can anyone tell me something special about Princess Marie—where she came from? How she knew about Jack?"

Mary waved her hand first. "Princess Marie had heard about the wonderful things Jack had done, so she decided to marry him," Mary said.

"But there are some very special things about Princess Marie," I said. "She lived in a most remarkable place. Does anyone have an idea where Princess Marie lived? Can you describe this place?"

Mary knew and was anxious to tell me, but as she had dominated the story to this point, I called on another child.

"Princess Marie lived in a castle surrounded by silver and gold trees," added Bobby.

"Yes," chimed in Mary, without being called on. "They were apple trees, and they grew silver and golden apples."

I wove this information into the tale, then asked, "How did Princess Marie know about Jack?"

Wendell raised his hand. "Everybody knew about Jack. He was rich and famous."

Mary added: "And when she decided to marry Jack, she got all dressed up in her best pink dress with ruffles. Her hair hung down in bouncy black curls. When she clapped her hands, silver horses came pulling a golden coach to take her to Jack's house."

Mary was rolling! Other children hardly had a chance to offer their own ideas. I wanted to block out the world and just play the game with Mary, letting her unhatch the whole new story. Mary's writing and reading skills may have been below grade level, but there was nothing wrong with her imagination or ability to articulate ideas.

"Who knows what happened when Princess Marie rode up to Jack's house in her golden coach?" I asked.

Emily volunteered. "When she got to Jack's house she said, 'This is Jack's house. I will knock on the door.' Jack answered. 'Who are you?' 'I am Princess Marie, and I came to marry you.' But Jack said, 'I don't really think I want to marry you.' Princess Marie said, 'Oh please do, I came so far.'"

"Who knows what Jack said then?" I asked. The children had taken charge of this unfolding story, now exhibiting a sense of ownership. I continued to weave and facilitate, keeping the flow going, reiterating their ideas.

Danny raised his hand. "Jack said, 'I will ask my mother. Mother, there is a girl out here—she says she wants to marry me. But I don't want to leave you.'"

"What did Jack's mother say then?" I asked.

Ellen piped up. "Jack's mother said, 'No, no, go marry her. I will stay home in this lonely house.' But Jack said, 'No, Mother, please come with me.'"

I wove in what the children contributed and our new "Jack and Princess Marie" ended this way:

Jack, Jack's mother, and Princess Marie returned to the castle, when Jack's mother said, "You aren't getting my Jack *that* easily, Princess Marie. You have to take three tests."

While the Princess was busy with her first test, scrubbing all the palace floors, she asked herself, "Do I really want Jack *that* badly?" "*Yes!*" she exclaimed.

Her second test was choosing which of two perfect roses was the *real* rose. A little bee flew into the real rose, telling her which one was real. (This information was contributed by a child who knew the story of how King Solomon solved a similar challenge by the Queen of Sheba. Later, Mrs. Theerman told me that this child was in the gifted program. Up to this point she had not raised her hand to contribute to the story.)

Princess Marie passed the third test by making a diary from the skin of a golden apple—using the core and stem for a lock and key.

Jack's mother said, "All right, you can have Jack." And they lived happily ever after.

Story weaving is exciting. The process is improvisational, and works best when there is a balance of power between story weaver and audience as they create the tale together. If story weavers see themselves as facilitating the process, the children see themselves as story creators. They sense ownership in the completed tale.

THE WRITING-READING CONNECTION

Following story weaving, classroom teachers coach their children who individually write, revise, edit, and polish their own original Jack Tales.

When I return the following week to Mrs. Theerman's class, I note that the children have set up a makeshift recording studio, to tape their stories. I am surprised at the variety of Jack Tales the children have composed.

Without a doubt, story weaving is a prewriting exercise that can motivate the most reluctant of students. For children such as Mary, with weak reading and writing skills, prodding her to write her version of the story "Jack and Princess Marie" is an easy task. Although Mary's written story was not as long, as detailed, or as involved as the oral rendering, she captured the essence of the new story to which she had contributed so much. She fluently read her version into the tape. This did not surprise me. Remedial reading students frequently read their own writing well, especially when it emerges from a process such as story weaving.

Children who have more developed skills often write complete pages, astonishing their teachers. Jane, an average student, surprised Mrs. Theerman by writing a four page Jack Tale, all in one paragraph, but filled with lush detail and description with perfect punctuation. What a way to evaluate a child's understanding of punctuation, grammar, and sentence structure, I thought. Jane might need some more understanding of paragraphing, but she certainly knows how to use quotation marks, and demonstrates an understanding of story.

"This story-writing process really stirred something in Jane," Mrs. Theerman observed. "Her writing was probably the most outstanding work that Jane had accomplished thus far in school. Until the children wrote their own Jack Tales, Jane seemed an average child. She didn't stand out in class. I was amazed that Jane stuck with the revision process until she had a fine story of which she could be proud."

When all the children had read their stories into the tape recorder, they listened attentively to their peers as the stories were replayed for them.

The children continued polishing their Jack Tales, finally illustrating and publishing them in accordion-folded books designed by Mrs. Theerman (see Appendix C).

Another teacher, June Von Weise, had children create beautiful illustrations for their Jack Tales by brushing a multicolored watercolor wash on sheets of 8 1/2" x 11" white paper. When these sheets dried, children used them to cut out their illustrations. Other children made illustrations from torn construction paper, or from collages from newspaper and magazine artwork.

JACK TALE STORY QUILTS: ART/ LANGUAGE ARTS EXTENSION

In another class, art instructor Sue Hinkel helped students design and construct a paper story quilt of the children's Jack Tales that was inspired by Faith Ringgold's books *Tar Beach* and *Dinner at Aunt Connie's*. (Ms. Ringgold's book illustrations are based on actual fabric quilts which she fashions from story themes.)

Using geometric shapes cut from colored paper, Hinkel showed how to make 12" by 12" squares reminiscent of traditional American quilt patterns. When the paper squares were complete, Hinkel asked the class to make another 12" by 12" paper square illustrating their individual Jack Tales. Hinkel and the children glued the squares, contrasting those that had geometric designs with those that told stories, onto large reinforced paper panels, creating one large story quilt. The paper quilt was displayed in the school hallway.

DRAMA, MATH, SOCIAL STUDIES

As news of the Jack Tale Unit spread, teachers from other grade levels asked to participate. As they did, exercises in drama, math, and social studies were added to the unit.

A Jack Drama: Characterization Through Movement

Drama games that used movement and pantomime exercises led children to a deeper level of understanding of characterization. In a game called Moving Characters (see Appendix B), children sit in a large circle around the work/play space. Children take turns entering the space to pantomime a character from the story; classmates guess who it is, what the action is, and when and where in the story it is taking place.

After listening to "Jack and the Beanstalk," one third grade class played Moving Characters in the Work/Play Space, an area in the classroom cleared of desks where designated movement and drama work takes place. Ronald jumped into the circle and moved catlike, arching his back, curling fingers like claws, snarling and pouncing with spring in his steps. Children in the class looked toward me, puzzled. "There's no cat in 'Jack and the Beanstalk,'" they whispered.

Initially, I am irritated with Ronald, who often tests me by stretching rules we have agreed upon. But the cat Ronald portrays is wonderful. When I ask Ronald if he is playing the giant's cat, he turns a somersault, shaking his head No. It is a beautiful response. I sense a golden moment. Can Ronald sustain his concentration and characterization? Can we keep this patch of dramatic play going?

"Are you the giant's wife's cat?" asks Melanie. Ronald licks a paw, then curls into a ball. A clue. I side-coach Melanie to enter the space as the giant's wife, urging her to talk quietly to the cat. "Here, Kitty, Kitty," she says, entering the play space. Ronald creeps toward her; he allows Melanie to pat his head. "Would you like some milk?" she asks. He nods. Melanie pantomimes the milk delivery; Ronald drinks the milk with a simulated cat tongue.

Side coaching occurs when the teacher or leader momentarily stops an exercise to make suggestions or give directions to help students deepen their awareness or appreciation of an activity in progress. When the scene is over, we praise Ronald for his playful role as the giant's wife's cat. Why did you play a cat when no cat was in the story? we asked. He said, "A cat should have been in the story. The giant was mean. He had the gold, the hen, and the harp. All the giant's wife had was hard work. She needed a friend."

Each time a student like Ronald makes a key contribution by changing or expanding the rules, I see how necessary it is to let these exercises flow and change. When I let go and allow the children to playfully take over, I signal to them that I respect their ideas. For the moment, we are partners in the process of creative play. When I don't let go, opportunities that could lead to original work are quite often missed.

There is a delicate balance between maintaining control and allowing fresh ideas to take us in new directions. Releasing control is at the heart of improvisation.

But letting go can be scary. It means leaving one's comfort zone to trust and risk, or shedding a traditional teaching style and slipping into a facilitator role.

Dramatic Play and Social Studies

In one fourth-grade class Jack Drama grew from a discussion of how the dead giant's body inconvenienced neighboring farmers in the English countryside. As the giant fell, the tale goes, various body parts crushed beehives, pigsties, village wells, chicken coops, and sheds. Miraculously, nobody was killed. Neighbors gathered in the village square to tell the constable how the giant's dead body had damaged their land. The complaints were so boisterous that the constable had to yell for "Order in the court!" Then, the teacher pointed to various citizens who took turns describing what had happened to their property. Finally, the crowd decided that they all should go to Jack's house and tell him of their losses in person.

The pair who played Jack and his mother listened to the charge that it was Jack's fault that the giant had fallen from the sky, causing untold destruction. They demanded that Jack pay damages. Again, the noise level was high as the scene took on aspects of a mob. The constable, played by an assertive girl, jumped on a chair and again demanded silence. She asked those who wished to make a formal complaint to address Jack and his mother.

Stopping the action, I side-coached Jack and his mother to go inside their imaginary hut and discuss the accusations of the people. They improvised a dialogue. When they returned, Jack and his mother faced the crowd: "What's your complaint?" they asked. One by one, villagers and farmers described their losses.

It was decided that villagers and farmers would put their complaints and expenses in writing. By now we were out of time, but it was a good place to stop the dramatic play. Besides, we were at a place to transition into Jack Math.

Math

During the math extension, the children retained their roles as villagers and farmers as they added up the repair costs of their damaged property. They prepared their complaints, complete with detailed accountings of losses and repair estimates, in letter form and delivered them to Jack and his mother.

As the exercise progressed in subsequent class sessions, the children worked in pairs. They played Jack and his mother, discussing between them how best to settle the claims. They wrote letters back to the farmers and villagers with their decisions.

Jack Math occurred in various ways. In some classes, it was decided that since the gold had been taken to the bank, repair payments could be partially paid from earned interest. Such problems led to a study of the price of gold on the world market, and how interest helps an investment grow. In other classes, Jack and his mother coaxed an overworked hen into laying an extra golden egg to pay the debts. Classmates were asked to decide how much Jack's golden eggs weighed, then how much each was worth based on the price of gold per ounce. Only then would Jack know how many eggs he needed to pay damages to the angry villagers.

Since Jack and his mother were afraid of being sued, they paid what they owed. However, if Jack had refused to pay, a mock trial could have been another "Jack" extension.

Jack Math/Science/Social Studies

In another classroom the children determined that the giant's body must be removed by dragging it to the sea. After assessing the giant's weight, determining how much rope and how many horses would be needed to haul the body, the class decided the project was too complicated. The upshot: a decision to leave the giant's body where it was, stuff it, hoist it up, and, of all things, convert it into an amusement park, complete with roller coaster, and a restaurant on top of the giant's head. Some discussed how fulcrums and pulleys could help hoist him upright; others weighed problems of taxidermy.

Although most children believed that a Giant Amusement Park would benefit the economy of the region, there were environmental concerns. What about pollution? Or a water and sewage system? What about bed and breakfasts for the tourists, and shops to provide services? But the local farming community changed due to the commercial venture, which concerned some citizens who liked things the way they were.

Since "Jack" is an English fairy tale, one social studies unit featuring Jack led to studies of the monarchy and aristocracy. Map studies pinpointed England, its link with the European continent, and surrounding bodies of water. England's special problems as an island country were focused on: farming practices; colonies; products, markets, shipping; weather; history; castles; traditions.

What if a contemporary Jack received five magic beans? How would the subsequent Jack Tales reflect current problems in England, similar to or different from those we face in the United States? Such a study could include the long relationship between England and America, leading to a study of colonial America as well as present-day issues and problems between the two countries.

LANGUAGE ARTS

Although the language arts are integral to most subject areas, a literature component of the Jack Tale unit involves reading other versions of "Jack and the Beanstalk." Richard Chase's *Jack Tales,* Donald Davis's *Jack Always Seeks His Fortune: Authentic Stories About Jack,* and Gail Haley's *Jack and the Fire Dragon* are Jack variants carried to Appalachia by English, Scottish, and Irish immigrants in the eighteenth and nineteenth centuries.

Jack Tales: A Book of Activities for Children

As the children wrote, revised, and edited their original Jack Tales and converted them to illustrated books, the teachers and I compiled a Jack Tale Activity Book based on exercises from our classroom experiences. This book included Jack math problems, language arts games that stimulated inventive thinking, and science projects such as growing beans and making bean recipes. In the book were blank pages on which the children could write, draw, and create maps. Here are examples of some activities:

- Create menus of the giant's favorite meals.
- Make up Mrs. Giant's favorite recipes.
- Draw pictures of the giant's strange pets.
- Make a map of the sky where the giant lived.
- Make a map of Jack's neighborhood.
- Design a castle—create it with rolls of newspaper and glue, construction paper and tissue paper.
- Write about how the giant's wife survives without him.
- Draw Jack's house before and after he became wealthy.

- Write another sequel to "Jack and the Beanstalk."
- Grow different kinds of beans in window pots.

The school district print shop "published" these Jack Tale Activity Books; copies went to each child participating in the unit as well as to school board members. Jack Tale books were displayed in the central office.

The Project TELL office began receiving phone calls from teachers of other grade levels and from other school districts who wanted more storytelling in their classrooms—all kinds of storytelling. Several teachers requested "Jack." As teachers from K through 5 adapted extension activities according to their students' ability levels and interests, we discovered that students of all ages enjoyed playing with "Jack."

STORYTELLING ACROSS THE CURRICULUM

Once teachers and students taste the elixir of using storytelling to stimulate learning, it is difficult to return to mere textbook-centered classrooms, with subject areas taught at specific times and topics of study thematically separated from each other. This integrated approach to teaching demonstrated by the Jack Tale unit is exhilarating, but not easy.

Story-centered learning is relatively inexpensive to pursue. No new texts or expensive computer programs are needed. Integrated curriculum design relies on teachers' seeing the possibilities for stories and storytelling to connect content in natural, inventive ways. Input from children for directions a particular unit might take is essential for its success. Children and teachers, working with the librarian, media and arts specialists, parent and community volunteers, all become storytellers in this unfolding pursuit of knowledge. Story, in its many guises, is at the heart of the curriculum, regardless of the content of the subject area.

2

Frog and Toad's Garden
Storytelling, Drama, Science, Poetry

Adaptable for Grades One Through Three

Dr. Belinda Wilucki (Ms. B) is a first-grade teacher whose mission is to instill the love of reading and learning in her children. Over the years we have created many units linking language arts and literature with science through storytelling, drama, and movement.

We begin our collaboration by sifting through her rich collection of picture books and texts. Although Ms. B uses a literature-based curriculum, she enjoys teaching from her collection of well-illustrated scientific picture books.

"Folktales, fairy tales, stories about other children or people are great for helping students appreciate many cultures," said Ms. B. "They teach values and serve to bridge language arts and social studies. But I am increasingly fascinated with picture books that teach science and math concepts."

Ms. B asked if we could combine storytelling and movement with a science unit, using "The Garden" from Arnold Lobel's *Frog and Toad Together.* "The children could study the nature of seeds and how they change as they grow into flowers and vegetables," she said. "I'll give the children some background by having them read *The Carrot Seed* by Ruth Krauss and Lois Ehlert's picture books on gardens. We can do some research on seeds."

I trust Ms. B's creativity and resourcefulness, confident that she will draw on ideas from her first graders as the unit develops. Teaching this way is invigorating. You start with an idea and a flexible framework and watch it evolve day by day.

During my first visit, the children were anxious to share poetry they had memorized and to tell about stories they had read on growing flowers and vegetables. Seed catalogs were visible on desks. A garden scene mural hung on the wall; it had been painted and labeled by the children.

Arnold Lobel's *Frog and Toad* stories, written for beginning readers as part of Harper and Row's I Can Read series, are deceptively simple. Frog and Toad, though best friends, often argue, disagree, and tackle problems that require creative solutions. Stories about Frog and Toad show that relationships are not always easy, often needing patience and understanding to work through conflict and disagreement.

THE GARDEN

In "The Garden," Toad insists he wants a garden like Frog's, regardless of Frog's warning that making a garden is "hard work." Toad goes home, digs his garden, and plants seed that Frog has given him.

Impatient, Toad yells at his seeds to start growing. Hearing noise, Frog comes running. He is angry with Toad, telling him he has frightened his seeds and that's why they won't grow. Toad, afraid he's scared his seeds to death, tells the seeds a story, sings them a song, reads them a poem. Still they don't grow. Finally, exhausted, Toad falls asleep in his garden. Frog comes and wakes Toad, telling him the good news: "Look, your garden has started growing."

"The Garden" lends itself to participatory, improvisational storytelling. This is a technique by which the storyteller invites the audience to contribute bits of information as the story is being told. Sometimes the storyteller cues the audience to sing a song or join in a call and response at a particular moment in the story. Participatory storytelling is different from story weaving, in which storyteller and audience make up the story as they go along.

Participatory Storytelling

In *participatory storytelling* the storyteller invites the audience to join in the story at some point, in some way: singing a song, echoing a chant, repeating certain phrases. The storyteller remains in control of the story being told, inviting the audience to participate during certain structured moments during the telling.

At the point in "The Garden" where Frog gives Toad seeds, I ask the class what kinds of seeds are to be planted. Ms. B's first graders chose carrots, tomatoes, lettuce, and spinach. When Toad shouts at the seeds to grow, Ms. B's children compose a cheer, which we chant together as part of the telling.

Grow, Seeds, Grow
Grow, Seeds Grow
Grow, Seeds,
Grow, Seeds,
Grow, Grow, Grow.

When Toad's seeds still don't grow, Toad sings to them. Marilyn, one of Ms. B's first graders, suggests *"Twinkle, Twinkle, Little Star,"* which we sing. In the story Toad writes a poem for the seeds. Barbara volunteers the first line; Michael adds a second and we all repeat it:

When the seeds
begin to grow
the birds will sweetly
sing to them.

No luck; the seeds still won't grow. Toad then tells the seeds a story. Someone suggests *"Jack and the Beanstalk."* The children take turns telling bits of "Jack" to encourage Toad's seeds to sprout.

No luck still. The seeds refuse to grow. Discouraged and exhausted, Toad falls asleep in his garden. Frog returns and shakes him: "Hey Toad, wake up and look!" Sure enough, the seeds have finally decided to grow. "You were right, Frog," says Toad, "growing a garden is very hard work."

Ms. B takes notes on everything the children contribute to the story to be used as material for writing a collaborative Big Book the children will make. Contents of the book include:

- the chant: "carrots, tomatoes, lettuce and spinach"
- a cheer: "Grow, seeds, grow!"
- short version of *"Jack and the Beanstalk"*
- the song: *"Twinkle, Twinkle, Little Star"*
- the poem

But first, the children want to "act it out."

Movement and Creative Drama Extensions

In their work/play space for movement exercises, the class pantomimes preparing the earth for planting by digging in the dirt, breaking clumps with imaginary hoes, smoothing lumps with rakes, and planting rows of carrot, tomato, lettuce, and spinach seeds.

Next, the children choose what kinds of vegetables they want to be, first imagining themselves as seeds planted in the earth. They take turns playing Toad, and cajole the seeds to grow by shouting, singing, telling a story, reciting a poem. But nothing works. The seeds refuse to grow.

Calling time out from dramatic play, we talked about what assistance seeds need in order to grow. Marty said they require worms and ants to soften the soil. Ms. B introduces the word *aerate,* and she and the children discuss how worms and other insects make air space in the dirt so water can seep in to soften the seeds for sprouting. Again playing the story, several children became wiggly worms, ants, and beetles—"aerating" the soil alongside the children playing sprouting seeds.

Ronnie wants to be the rain; Margaret, the sun; Emily, the moon, since seeds grow at night, too. Bruce said what was needed most of all was patience. Children playing seeds begin to grow. They take turns playing Toad.

As the seeds sprout, Frog comes and shakes an exhausted, sleeping Toad. "Wake up, Toad, your seeds are growing!" Jubilantly, Frog and Toad dance and jump among the seedlings; worms and ants continue to aerate the soil; Margaret, as the sun, shines; Ronnie rains.

After a lively finale, I hit the drum, a cue to stop the action. "Look!" "What a lovely rainbow. The sun came out during the rain shower." The class applauds the sight of the imaginary rainbow. It is the end of a successful storytelling and movement exercise.

Often I tell teachers who want to begin using creative drama and movement in their classrooms, "Close the door; pull down the shade, hang a DO NOT DISTURB: TESTING sign on the door."

Children do get noisy, but with patience, practice, and a hand drum to cue FREEZE or SILENCE, order returns just when everything seems out of hand. A little joyful noise is natural to the playful process of inventive problem solving during creative movement. A story such as "The Garden" provides a strong framework to ease teachers into bridging storytelling with creative drama in their classrooms.

Science

I stayed to evaluate the session with Ms. B. and to plan the next step. She thought it would be excellent reinforcement to ask the class to plant carrots, tomatoes, lettuce, and spinach in peat pots and to chart their growth.

By my next visit, peat pots were on the windowsills. In groups, the children were asked to chart:

- Which plant sprouted first?
- Which grew fastest?
- How much water do plants require?
- What time of day does sunlight "feed" seeds through the window?
- How much sun are the plants getting?

By my next visit the seeds had not started growing. I suggested we chant, "Grow, seeds, grow!" "Oh, no, we'll scare them to death," giggled Timothy. "We could chant it quietly," suggested Megan. So we did.

We sang *"Twinkle, Twinkle, Little Star."* The children didn't want to tell the seeds the story of *"Jack and the Beanstalk."* "It's too long," groaned Anthony. But Margaret found a poem about seeds; she recited it.

Writing and Reading Connections

Ms. B unhooked a Big Book hanging from a rack under the blackboard. "Maybe Mrs. Rubright would like to hear you read the Big Book you wrote as a group based on the *Frog and Toad* story from last week."

Scrambling to their seats, the children were soon reading their version of "The Garden" in unison as Ms. B turned the pages of the Big Book they had collaboratively written and illustrated.

The class showed me their own individually written and illustrated books of their versions of "The Garden," soon to be taken home and shared with parents.

FROM STORY TO POETRY WRITING

One February, Ms. B. and her first graders were deep into winter themes that related to topics in math and science: how ice is made, and melts; what snow is; charting the lengthening days; why seasons change; and the arrival of spring. When she invited me and Constance Levy, a poet, to visit to do storytelling and poetry writing, we discovered our visit would occur on Groundhog Day. Ms. B said, "Great! I'll have the children do some research on groundhogs and the folklore of Groundhog Day."

During the story-weaving session the children and I made up a humorous story about a groundhog who was scared by his shadow and retreated into his burrow to sleep through another six weeks of winter. The story was full of images of farm animals enduring a cold and snowy winter: scruffy-coated horses, fluffy, woolly lambs, mud-cloaked pigs in need of a spring scrubbing.

Mrs. Levy and I returned the following week to listen to Ms. B's children read their groundhog stories. Mrs. Levy shared favorite poems on winter themes from Jack Prelutsky's anthology *The Random House Book of Poetry for Children.* Then she read Nikki Giovanni's "Winter Poem," Dorothy Aldis's "On a Snowy Day," Marchette Chute's "Snowflakes," "Snow and Spring" by Ivy O. Eastwick, and "Song" by Ruth Kraus, which is full of luscious images children can feel and hear as snow melts on a sunny winter day.

(Mrs. Levy always comes to her poetry sessions with a satchel of poems, appropriate to the topic the children are studying. She believes that the secret to helping children fall in love with poetry is to read poems to them. Lots and lots of poems.)

"If we are going to write about what it feels like to walk in the snow, we'd better take a snow walk first," Mrs. Levy says.

The children, with Mrs. Levy in their midst, pantomime a walk through heavy snow. As they move they chant slowly a line from "Snow Feet," a poem from her book *I'm Going to Pet a Worm Today.*

> *A snow walk's a slow walk*
> *When snow drifts are deep*

Following the "winter walk" pantomime, Mrs. Levy said, "You know, I still remember the poem I wrote about snowflakes when I was in first grade."

> *I saw a little speck of white*
> *come falling to the ground.*

I thought it was a feather
for it didn't make a sound.

Then more and more came falling
'til they were all around.

Now I know they were snowflakes
and not feathers falling down.

"Now it's time for you to write your own poems." She asks: "What does the sun feel like on a winter day?"

The children call out suggestions, which Ms. B lists on the board:

"Like you're home sitting in front of a heater."

"Like hot fudge poured over ice cream."

Chris says, "The sun feels like a cherry pie right out of the oven." Mrs. Levy says, "Chris, that's a poem. Just as it is! Look!" she says as Ms. B. writes Chris's poem on the board.

Sun Feelings

The Sun
feels like a
cherry pie
right out of the oven.

    By CHRIS

Ms. B's first graders rush to contribute their ideas. The children debate which mental pictures they like best. Their word and phrase choices become the raw material from which Mrs. Levy and the class mix and match images that turned into simple, short group poems.

Snowflakes

Snowflakes
are
marshmallows
tumbling
tumbling
tumbling
down.

    By IAN and KAM

Snowflakes

Snowflakes
are
little snowballs.
Maybe the cloud
ants are
having a fight.

By DWAYNE and ZACHERY

Baby Clouds

Snowflakes
are teensy
clouds
floating
from the big
clouds.

By COLLEEN

Snowflakes

Snowflakes
are like
spider webs
in the sky

They fall
like the wind blows the leaves.
They bounce down.

Or like smoke
coming from a chimney
they turn
and twist
and twirl.

By SALLY, STEPHEN, CHRIS, and DARRELL

Snowflakes

Falling
like cotton floating down
they hit the ground softly

like a feather
like a bird lands—

not like a meteor would land
like a bomb
not like an airplane which would
land bumpily
not like a whale who lands
with a splash.

By STEPHANIE, JOSIE, CHRIS, IAN, MIKE, and SALLY

The snowflake poems were completed during Mrs. Levy's one-hour poetry session. Ms. B transcribed the poems into booklets for her first graders to read and take home.

Reflecting on what the children learned during our sessions together, Ms. B. said, "Science concepts were reinforced through storytelling, dramatic play, and poetry. The children demonstrated their growing literacy by articulating their ideas, and expanding their oral and written language skills. There is no formula, or right way to teach this way. All that is necessary is to relinquish control and follow the lead of the children. When teachers exercise a little imagination and are willing to be open and try different approaches, amazing things happen in the classroom."

3

Rosie's Walk
An Interdisciplinary Approach

Adaptable for Pre-school Through
Grade Three

Pat Hutchins's classic picture book, *Rosie's Walk*, is a springboard to improvisational games that can spawn the creation of original stories and yield numerous interdisciplinary curricular extensions. Hutchins's thirty-nine-word narrative describes some encounters of Rosie the hen as she takes a farmyard walk. Illustrations in the book portray the troubles of the unfortunate fox who is in futile pursuit of Rosie for his dinner.

Unaware she is being pursued, Rosie stumbles past a raft of farm-yard obstacles on her way safely home. Meanwhile, the fox, smacked on the nose by a rake, soggy from a fall into the lake, hay covered, smothered by a broken sack of flour, chased by angry bees, finally retreats into the deep dark woods—without his chicken dinner! With a cast of two characters and broadly developed tensions, *Rosie's Walk* is a catalyst to provide a framework for playing with new ideas and bringing them to life with drama and creative writing.

ROSIE'S WALK "TEACHES" READING

The degree to which a child can predict what might happen to the fox on his walk reveals how well that child can infer from the book's illustrations what will happen next to the fox. Children's perceptions and predictions help teachers judge the class's level of reading readiness.

Telling the story *before* the children actually see the book—using chant and movement—is a tactic to assist the class in understanding the story bones: the sequence of events, setting, characters, and outcome. Now they are free to explore other dimensions of the story through sound and movement.

Storytelling and Chant

In the voice of a squawking chicken, changing tempo, pitch, intensity, —and interspersing a chant, WALK, WALK, WALK, WALK—the storyteller narrates Rosie's walk around the farm. Following the storytelling, a movement game, Chicken Aerobics, is introduced.

Chicken Aerobics

Chicken Aerobics lets children play with chickenlike movements. From auditory cues on a hand drum, children isolate and move their arms like chicken wings, their legs like chicken legs, their torsos like chicken middles, and their feet as if they were chickens scratching for food. Moving heads, arms, torsos, and legs together, as do real chickens, the class moves about the work/play area (hen yard) clucking and pecking for food. Moving left, right, backward, forward, in circles, up and down, fast and slow, high and low, children develop a movement vocabulary.

Next, imagining that they are foxes on the prowl for a chicken dinner, the class moves through space that simulates a farmyard. The storyteller—a teacher or pupil—narrates the story; the class acts it out, alternately as chickens or foxes.

Playing Out the Story

In small groups, children construct a hen house, a pond, a haystack, a mill, a gate, and bee hives using their bodies to make the shapes. As a student narrates the tale, children playing the roles of a chicken and a fox move through, around, between, over, and under the various farm sites that their peers are creating with their intertwined arms and legs.

Retelling from a Different Point of View

Retelling the story from the perspective of the fox, employing words beginning with *S,* classmates picture the fox at junctions in the story where his pursuit of Rosie as dinner victim is foiled. Examples of words introduced by a typical class are:

stealthy	stammering	straying
silent	staring	strange
slippery	stately	striking
sneaky	stationary	stupid
slithery	staunch	stuck-up
starving	stirring	stubborn
stalking	stretching	stumbling
staggering		

Playing with *S* words is an opportunity for teachers to teach alliteration, enrich vocabularies, build dictionary and thesaurus skills, and accent grammar and spelling. A discussion follows on how adjectives help one better understand and describe a character such as the unfortunate fox.

LARGE GROUP STORY WEAVING

A large group collaboration with one person, a teacher or volunteer, as story weaver, blends in ideas and suggestions offered by the group. An example of such story weaving to create a sequel to *Rosie's Walk* follows.

Frederick's Mane

Something unusual was going on with a group of fifteen six- and seven-year-olds at a Young Writer's Conference in Iowa City. My job was to demonstrate the story-weaving process for teachers and parents. After listening to *Rosie's Walk*, the students could hardly wait to construct their own story about a chicken called Henrietta. I had never seen such enthusiasm for inventive thinking triggered through story weaving. What was going on? I realized that the Iowa City children possessed a powerful sense of ownership of the unfolding tale. They saw themselves as authors confident in their own ideas.

I expected the conference director, Dr. Bill Lyons, to tell me that the students represented the district's gifted and talented program. "Not at all," he replied. "Most schools choose students from a random draw of names of those who have expressed an interest in attending."

During story weaving, I stress that children must listen to ideas their peers contribute, visualize how such ideas fit into the developing tale, then adjust their own ideas to the changing story. Needless to say, the students were passionate about their ideas; they wanted them all included.

Their ideas were not only substantial, they were humorous as well. Dramatic play occurred spontaneously when the students jumped up to take turns playing in the developing story: cat, sheep, cow, dog, Henrietta the hen, and Frederick the horse.

The resultant improvisational story, "Frederick's Mane," was boisterous and funny with inventive dialogue and animal sounds. By modeling the process, I hoped that teachers and parents observing the technique would try story weaving in their classrooms or their own homes in similar ways.

Here is the story the Iowa City first- and second-grade students created:

Henrietta Hen wanted to visit Frederick the horse, but Frederick wasn't in the barn. He wasn't in the pasture, either. He was nowhere to be found.

Henrietta asked the cat, "Have you seen Frederick?" "No, I haven't seen him," replied the cat, "but I hear his mane is blue."

"No!" said Henrietta.

"It's true. Frederick the horse has a mane that is blue."

"How do you know? Did you see him with your own eyes?" asked Henrietta.

"Well, no," said the cat, "I didn't actually see him, but I heard that he stuck his head in a bucket of blue paint, thinking it was water. When he tried to wash his head in the pond, the blue paint didn't come off his mane. Since he's nowhere to be found, Frederick must be hiding."

"Who told you this?" asked Henrietta.

"A little mouse told me," said the cat, licking his whiskers.

"Oh sure," mumbled Henrietta. "A nervous mouse would tell a cat anything."

Henrietta visited Mrs. Sheep. "Have you seen Frederick?" she asked.

"Well, I haven't actually seen him," said Mrs. Sheep. "But I hear he's covered with blue paint. Imagine a blue horse!" Mrs. Sheep laughed so heartily that Mrs. Cow strolled over to find out why.

When Mrs. Sheep told Mrs. Cow what she was laughing about, Mrs. Cow chuckled. "I heard that the paint was in a bucket hanging on the ladder leaning against the barn. And when it fell on Frederick's head he reared up and the bucket landed on his back and dribbled paint down his tail."

Mrs. Sheep and Mrs. Cow laughed and laughed.

"I hear he's gone into hiding," said Henrietta, wondering what was the truth about Frederick.

The dog ran over to see what the noise was about. Mrs. Sheep and Mrs. Cow told him about Frederick's blue mane and tail.

"I heard all about it," barked the dog. "The rooster said Frederick is so embarrassed, he's hiding under the farmer's porch. But he doesn't quite fit." The dog howled. The sheep baa'd. The cow mooed.

Henrietta clucked: "Well, I don't think all this is so funny. Besides, I know the rooster and he will tell you anything you want to hear. Believe me, I know."

A black crow landed on a fence post. "Caw! Caw! Frederick's hiding, all right. I just saw him among the high stalks in the cornfield, trotting toward town."

"You *saw* him?" Henrietta asked the crow. "Did he have a blue mane and tail?"

"Couldn't tell, couldn't tell," cawed the crow, flying off.

"Now why would Frederick be trotting toward town?" wondered Mrs. Cow.

"Maybe he's running away because you all were laughing at him," said Henrietta. "Come on!" she commanded. Followed by the cat, sheep, cow, and dog, Henrietta took off hopping, jumping, flying toward the large cornfield that reached to the edge of town. No one was laughing now. "Spread out!" ordered Henrietta. "If he's in this cornfield, we'll find him."

Henrietta clucking, the cat meowing, the dog barking, the sheep bleating, and the cow mooing—all were noisily calling Frederick.

Frederick didn't hear a thing as he trotted into town. At the barber shop on Main Street, Frederick stopped and looked inside. Surprised at the sight of Frederick, the customers ran outside to look at the horse with a blue mane and tail. As they did so, Frederick trotted inside and sat down in a barber's chair.

"Hey! You can't do that," yelled the barber. Frederick swished his mane to and fro. "You want your blue mane cut off?" asked the barber. Frederick nodded. The barber cut off Frederick's mane, then rubbed his neck with sweet-smelling lotion.

Frederick whinnied thanks. He got up. His tail swished in the barber's face. "Hey! You want me to cut off your tail, too?" Frederick nodded. So, the barber cut off Frederick's tail and tied a blue ribbon on the stub.

Frederick bowed to the barber. The other customers applauded as Frederick pranced out of the shop. By now Henrietta Hen and the animals were at the edge of the cornfield. "Frederick is nowhere to be found," Henrietta said.

"Long gone, long gone," cawed the crow from overhead.

"Frederick ran away because we laughed at him," said Mrs. Sheep, sadly.

"Look!" cried Henrietta, pointing her wing toward the road. "It's Frederick! He's coming home!" Frederick ambled toward the cornfield. "He doesn't have a blue mane; he doesn't have a blue tail. But he does have a blue ribbon tied to what's left of his tail. He looks fine," said Henrietta.

Mrs. Sheep looked sheepish; Mrs. Cow looked sheepish; the cat and dog looked sheepish. Frederick did not look sheepish; neither did Henrietta. She turned around and shook a wing at her friends. "See what happens when you spread rumors? You make everybody look foolish."

The animals pointed accusing paws and hooves at each other:

The dog said, "The rooster said—"

The rooster said, "The cat said—"

The cow said, "The dog said—"

The sheep said, "The cow said—"

The cat said, "The mouse said—"

Everyone stared at the cat, who said, "It was the mouse who told me that Frederick had a blue mane." But the mouse who had seen it all could say nothing because he had been eaten for breakfast by the cat. "The eyewitness is gone; nobody can prove a thing," said Henrietta.

"Now that all the fuss is over, Frederick," said Henrietta, "may I have a ride back? I'm pooped."

Frederick leaned his head low to the ground. Henrietta marched up over his head, sliding across the stubble of Frederick's shaved mane. "Hummm! You do smell good, Frederick," Henrietta whispered. "You would never believe what everyone was saying about you today."

But Frederick said nothing. Prancing proudly, he led the parade of animals back into the farmyard.

If spreading rumors and gossiping was the theme of this story, Henrietta's loyalty to Frederick, and her determination to solve the blue mane mystery, were important also. Her sensitivity to Frederick's embarrassment was evident, too.

It didn't surprise me that these young children naturally seemed to understand issues of fairness and honesty. One little boy asked whether Frederick *really* had a blue mane and tail. "What do you think?" I responded. He said, "I think Henrietta asked Frederick when nobody else was around, and he told her the truth."

"What do you think was the truth?" I asked.

"That blue paint had fallen on his mane and tail; that he was embarrassed and the barber cut them off."

The story-weaving exercise that generated "Frederick's Mane" is an example of a prewriting activity that generates inventive thinking and speaking skills. When it's time to commit the story to paper, rarely does anyone say, "I don't have anything to write about."

Dr. Lyons says that if the children wrote their own versions of "Frederick's Mane," they would use "process writing," a series of steps a piece of writing must go through before it is considered polished. Steps in the writing process developed by Iowa City teachers are called STAR:

S—Subtract unnecessary words.
T—Transpose material by moving it around.
A—Add material.
R—Replace lifeless words or revise by changing order of content.

ROSIE'S WALK: CONNECTIONS TO INTERDISCIPLINARY STUDIES

Rosie's Walk serves as a way to initiate discussion of farm life in different parts of the country. On a trip to Alaska, I asked about hens and chickens during a visit to John Rusyniak's classroom in the town of Circle. Rusyniak told me that generally chicken meat and eggs were expensive, almost a luxury, as they had to be imported from Seattle. Rusyniak's children, kindergarten through sixth grade, and

I played with *Rosie* to initiate interdisciplinary activities about farm life. Activities included elements of math and science.

After a session of creative drama, I said, "Let's draw Rosie's farm on the blackboard." Rusyniak, teacher and principal of the small school near the Arctic Circle, found colored chalk.

Six-year-old Marie fashioned the hen house, complete with a chimney that smoked, windows with flower boxes, and a pebble path.

Squeezed shoulder to shoulder at the board, classmates created a scene filled with birds, butterflies, bugs, frogs, turtles, and fish in the pond. One small boy, his fist clutching chalk, pounded the board to make dozens of tiny yellow points. "Bees, circling the hive," he explained.

One student produced a small log cabin with a garden that grew large heads of cabbage. The artist said, "These cabbages aren't as big as the ones grown in the Matanuska Valley outside of Anchorage, but we do grow cabbages up here, even if we are only thirty miles from the Arctic Circle." Mountain lakes, trout streams, caves for hibernating bears, and fox dens were added.

In the Alaskan class, one child added chicken tracks to the blackboard mural to show Rosie's trail; another made fox tracks to follow her. The mural was transformed into a map, perfect for studying direction—left, right, north, south, east, west.

How many steps did Rosie take to walk around the pond? If her entire walk lasted an hour, how long did it take Rosie to walk around, through, over, under, past, and between each site on her walk? How many leaps did the fox make to reach the haystack? How many more steps did it take Rosie to travel the same distance? If Rosie flew from site to site could she travel faster than the fox running? What makes you think so? All of these activities can be acted out by the class, extending math lessons into dramatic play.

In classrooms such as Rusyniak's, curriculum grows and develops, bridging content areas. Such classrooms become learning laboratories where teachers and students explore together.

"That's exactly how I teach. I have to," Rusyniak said, reflecting a commitment to experiential learning. "Although it isn't always easy having such a range of ages, the interaction between my students stretches the younger ones and helps the older children process and articulate what they have learned.

"Last week I got a call from a parent who had killed a moose up in a mountain pass. He asked if the class and I could help dress it and carry the meat down in small packs. My lesson plan that day called for creative writing, science, and physical education.

"We dropped everything and piled the children in Jeeps and took off to the mountain, where we hiked in three quarters of a mile to skin and dress the moose.

"The older children worked all day learning how to dress a moose. They used math in their measurement of packets of meat. They predicted how much weight each child could carry in packs, as well as the distance down the path to the truck. We wrote about what we did, including sharing family recipes for moose stew and sausage, and how we felt about the experience.

"My pupils are Athabascan, so the moose was butchered according to tribal custom. These children live close to nature. I have one boy who sets rabbit snares in the morning on his way to school and takes what he catches home for dinner after school.

"We try to connect what we teach in school to what is happening in their lives, preserving old cultural values."

"What did the younger children do when the older children were butchering the moose?" I asked.

"They gathered blueberries and assisted a mother, who had joined us, in tending a fire where our tea simmered in tin cans," said Rusyniak. Later the younger children helped the older children roast slices of fresh moose meat over the flame.

"Teachers need to have plans and curriculum designs, but more important, they need to discard them, or put them aside, if a more authentic learning opportunity appears at the spur of the moment," Rusyniak concluded. "Storytelling is natural to this process. My students reflect on what they have done; they talk and write about it."

4

Bellerophon and Pegasus
Storytelling and Movement

Adaptable for Grades Three Through Eight

When Ms. Tuley asked if I could help her third graders act out the Greek myth "Bellerophon and Pegasus the Winged Horse" using movement, I visualized her children pantomiming Pegasus, grazing and drinking from sweet water springs, then spreading their arms like wings and soaring into the Grecian sky, toward Mount Olympus. "But why don't you do this yourself?" I asked. "You are already known as a storytelling teacher in your building. Your rendering of your Thanksgiving turkey tale is famous."

"I know," she replied, "but I've never used movement in retelling the story like you sometimes do, and I'd like to watch how you do this before trying it myself."

When I arrived, the children had already pushed the desks against the wall, creating a work/play space in the center of the room. Before telling the story, Ms. Tuley asked the children to review Greek myths they had already read.

Marianne said, "We read about King Midas and how everything he touched turned to gold. Even his food, so he had nothing to eat." "Even his little daughter!" piped Melanie.

Tom said, "We also read about a girl named Atalanta who could beat all the boys in running races, but a boy tricked her in a race by throwing golden apples at her so she would stop to pick them up." "Yeah, he won and got to marry her, even though she didn't want to," added Mike.

During the discussion the children demonstrated they were aware of moral issues in the stories; they understood that behavior has consequences. Comparing and contrasting the stories of King Midas and Atalanta, they saw how greed and vanity led to the loss of something each loved. "Well, let's see what you discover in the story of Bellerophon and Pegasus," I said.

BELLEROPHON AND PEGASUS: A SYNOPSIS

Bellerophon, the trainer of horses, dreamed of capturing Pegasus, the flying horse. Traveling to the temple of Athena, Bellerophon fell asleep praying to the goddess for help. In a dream Bellerophon caught Pegasus and tamed him by throwing a golden bridle over his head. When Bellerophon woke up, a golden bridle was in his hands. He knew that Athena had answered his request.

One day, when Bellerophon was in Corinth, he saw Pegasus drinking from a stream. Flinging the golden bridle over his neck, Bellerophon jumped on the magnificent creature's back. "Fly," commanded Bellerophon. Pegasus obeyed. From that day Pegasus and Bellerophon were inseparable. They had many adventures together, including a battle with the terrible fire-breathing monster, Chimera.

Later in his life, Bellerophon became proud of his achievements. He thought he was as powerful as the gods. When he tried to ride Pegasus to Mount Olympus, an angry Zeus caused Pegasus to throw Bellerophon from his back. Falling to earth, Bellerophon landed on briars, and wandered as a lame beggar the rest of his life.

In class, the children discussed how pride could be as deadly as greed and vanity for getting folks into trouble. We talked about the old saying, "Pride goeth before a fall."

Brainstorming ways they could act out the story using movement, Ms. Tuley listed the children's ideas on the board:

Pegasus flying
Bellerophon lassos Pegasus
Bellerophon taming Pegasus with the golden bridle
Pegasus and Bellerophon soaring through the sky together
Chimera roaring, bellowing fire from his lion's mouth
Pegasus and Bellerophon battling the Chimera monster
Pegasus pitching Bellerophon through the air to land on briars
Bellerophon, lame, wandering as a beggar until he dies.

Each child found a spot in our work/play space and claimed it by swirling around in it, arms outstretched, shouting, "This is my space!" I remind the children not to invade another person's space unless the exercise calls for collaboration.

Pegasus (whole group working individually)

Working simultaneously in their individual spaces, (nonlocomotor), the children imagined they were Pegasus drinking from the cold spring using low-level movements. Arching and stretching arms like wings, they prepared for flight.

Cueing on a hand drum, I suggest that the children move through the room (locomotor) in slow motion, stretching wings, soaring into the air. Side coaching, I remind them to use different levels as they soar, circle, swoop, and dive—and to move in different directions: backward, forward, sideways, diagonally. Reminding them not to bump others playing Pegasus, I signal them to return to earth—enter their own space and settle down to rest.

Bellerophon (whole group working simultaneously)

The children, now playing Bellerophon, pantomime capturing Pegasus with a lasso (missing, catching him; feeling him tug, pull, yank; holding on). Side coaching helps them concentrate—seeing, feeling the rope as they catch an imaginary Pegasus who tries to escape by running, jumping, flying, pulling, tugging, yanking to get free.

Bellerophon and Pegasus (working in pairs)

While the rest of us serve as audience, pairs of children take turns sharing their interpretations of Bellerophon capturing Pegasus with an imaginary lasso.

A kind of "dance" evolves between pairs of children playing Bellerophon trying to capture Pegasus. The work of one pair of children stands out.

Fully engrossed in the exercise, each focuses on the movement of the other. A determined Bellerophon stalks a wary Pegasus. Now and again he flings an imaginary rope at the horse's neck. Pegasus eludes him. Finally, Bellerophon thrusts the rope at the exact right moment. Pegasus knows there is no escape. He lets the rope snare him.

The child playing Pegasus tugs, pulls, twists, and turns; the child who plays Bellerophon pulls harder on the imaginary rope. Briefly, everyone in the room *sees* the horse and captor struggling. The total concentration of these children made the scene come alive.

Ms. Tuley and I noted how when children become the characters, playing out the stories that they have heard told or read, they stretch all their senses. Vicariously, they see, smell, taste, touch, feel, hear what is in the tale, appreciating and understanding the story's meaning at a deep level because, in imagination, *they are there.*

Storytelling also serves as a memory device. Playing the tale out using movement imprints details of the story in memory, kinesthetically. When I meet former students years later they often say, "Remember the time you told that story and we acted it out?" They remember every detail.

5

The Sea
Movement, Stories, and Poetry

Adaptable for Grades Three Through Eight

Vera Karsch is a dancer. She is also a fifth-grade teacher who explores using movement in her classroom. "Up to now," she says to me, "I have used dance with my students in a very structured way for a specific purpose—like creating a pageant for Christmas or a special event. Can we brainstorm ways to incorporate movement into my everyday teaching . . . maybe helping my fifth-graders to use movement to make up stories?"

Ms. Karsch and I decided to use the Plate Dance, Space Walk, Underwater Walk, and Mirror Game to help students explore movement. After placing their chairs in a semicircle against the wall to create a work/play space in the all-purpose room, Karsch printed principles of movement on the board.

LEVELS	TEMPO	INTENSITY	DIMENSION	DIRECTION
high	fast	strong	large	backward
middle	slow	weak	small	forward
low		heavy		sideways
		light		diagonally

Then she and the children discussed many of the ways it is possible to move:

bending	leaping	soaring
contracting	marching	spreading
crawling	plopping	stomping

creeping	plunging	stretching
crouching	popping	striding
expanding	pulling	swaying
exploding	pushing	swirling
falling	shaking	tiptoeing
floating	shuffling	tripping
flying	skipping	turning
hopping	sliding	twirling
jumping	slithering	twisting

Karsch explained that dancers call these terms their *movement vocabulary*, using them in ways similar to authors who use word vocabularies to compose prose or poetry. "The games we play today will help you develop a movement vocabulary," she says.

PLATE DANCE (LARGE GROUP EXERCISE)

"Place yourselves evenly in the space. Put a paper plate under each foot. There are ten short musical selections from classical to rock on the audiotape," she explains. "Just move the way the music makes you feel, keeping your feet on the plates. Start moving in your own space (nonlocomotor). When I signal, feel free to move all around the room (locomotor). The only rule is: Don't invade another person's space. The Plate Dance is a warm-up to other movement activities we'll do today."

With paper plates under each foot, the children swirled, swished, turned, twisted, twirled, rocked, glided, and slid between and around one another. "Remember, use high, middle, and low levels," side-coaches Karsch. Laughing, sweating, out of breath when the music was over, they begged, "Let's do it again!" We did.

"Now I know why it's called a warm-up," sighs Jeremy as he plopped into his chair along with the other panting children. After a short rest the children were ready to play Space Walk.

SPACE WALK (LARGE GROUP EXERCISE)

In Space Walk children change movement levels, vary tempos, explore large and small dimensions, and play with qualities (smooth, jerky, strong, weak) as they move through different imaginary environments or substances: water, jello, peanut butter, dense jungle, outer space, bubbles, Ping-Pong balls.

Finally, we move through deep water.

UNDERWATER WALK (LARGE GROUP EXERCISE)

"Imagine you are walking on the bottom of the ocean floor wearing heavy underwater diving gear. What might you see?"

"Catfish, sharks, dolphins, whales, eels, octopuses, clams, seahorses, seaweed, coral," call the children.

"To the beat of the drum, become one of the objects mentioned, and move like you think that object moves through the water." There was no silliness. The children completely focused on the task.

MIRROR GAME (WORKING IN PAIRS)

Listening to synthesized music that includes strange sounds suggesting bubbles and gurgles, children play the mirror game in pairs. The person who is 'it' initiates movement of an underwater sea creature, while the partner mirrors the action in pantomime. The partners take turns leading the movement. Maintaining eye contact, the children's mirror movements suggest seaweed, giant clams opening and closing, crabs creeping over the ocean floor, octopuses twisting their arms.

A week later Karsch called to invite me to see the children's stories which they had choreographed using movement. She was delighted when I asked if I might bring poet Constance Levy to observe. Long ago, Connie and I discovered that listening to stories is one way to give children rich mental images from which to draw when they write poetry. Perhaps some poetry might come from Karsch's students' work with movement stories.

With surreal music providing the background, the groups took turns presenting their work. One group of girls entered the space single file from behind a bookcase swirling blue crepe-paper streamers. Their circular arm movements suggested giant fish fins and tails. A few children swayed like seaweed rooted in the sand, flowing around a small group of children who opened and closed their arms like giant clams as "fish" swam among them.

"Guess what we were," said Nancy when they had completed their dance. "You reminded me of a school of fish," I said.

"Could you see us swimming away from a giant clam? We entered a cave to escape being eaten." Next, a group of boys twirled through the space, suggesting a whirlpool, ending their scene scrunched together in a corner. "Looks like you were all caught in a net," I said. They beamed. "You're right. A fisherman's net!"

Three boys not interested in playing until the others had shared their group work now begged to have a turn. Karsch and I encouraged them to try. Hurriedly, they had a conference, grabbing blue crepe streamers as they talked.

I had little faith in the quality of work so quickly thrown together, but was surprised by what I saw. Each boy "swam" into the space from a different part of the room, twisting and turning, floating the streamers clutched in their hands over and under and around. Converging in the center of the space they battled and devoured some sort of sea creature before spinning off again, receding to the corners from which they had begun their piece. Their movement, free and spontaneous, was executed with sensitivity and imagination, applying all the movement principles we had worked on during the preceding weeks.

"It seems like you were attacking, and devouring some sort of creature, before swimming off again," I said. "It was a monster from the deep," chuckled Ian, proud of their spontaneous work.

The children happily plopped on the floor to rest. I told them that our visitor, Levy, the poet, often worked with children following storytelling or creative drama sessions to help students express their experiences through poetry.

Levy said, "Your movement was like poetry. It reminded me of a poem I brought by James Reeves (1994) called 'Grim and Gloomy.' It particularly fits the carnivorous mood of the last group's presentation." She read:

Grim and Gloomy

Oh, grim and gloomy,
So grim and gloomy
Are the caves beneath the sea.
Oh, rare but roomy
And bare and boomy,
Those salt sea caverns be.

Oh, slim and slimy
Or gray and grimy
Are the animals of the sea.
Salt and oozy
And safe and snoozy
The caves where those animals be.
Hark to the shuffling,

Huge and snuffling,
Ravenous, cavernous,
Great sea-beasts!
But fair and fabulous,
Tintinnabulous,
Gay and fabulous are their feasts.

Ah, but the queen of the sea,
The querulous, perilous sea!

How the curls of her tresses
Sway and swirl in the waves,
How cozy and dozy,
How sweet ring-a-rosy
Her bower in the deep sea caves!
Oh, rare but roomy
And bare and boomy
Those caverns under the sea,
And grave and grandiose,
Safe and sandiose
The dens of her denizens be.

POETRY WRITING (LARGE GROUP SESSION)

"Now I think it's time for you to write a poem based on your own underwater pantomimes," Levy said. She asked the children to search for just the right word to describe a feeling, a sense, or an image based on the movement stories they had just created. "Imagine seaweed—how it feels, looks, moves."

As the children bubble forth words, I write them on the board to create a word bank from which Levy will help the children write a group poem.

How seaweed:

LOOKS	FEELS	MOVES
curvy	slimy	swirly
nibbled at	tickly	tangly
twisted like rope	slippery	dancing

greenish	free	floating
brown and black	squirmy swaying	
transparent	swooshing	
	stretching	

Who uses seaweed?

eels
jellyfish
rainbow fish

What do they use it for?

munching for food
as a house
as camouflage
to hide in
to lurk in

Starting with the collection of words on the board, Levy helps the children play with words to create surprise images. This process led to the children's group poem, "Something."

Something

What is swaying in the sand?
Squirming eels and jelly fish.

What is splashing, swooshing, squashing
by the dancing water weeds?
What is stretching to reach the rainbow fish?
Something
crunching
grinding
chopping
its sharp
razor teeth.
Something.

"I think a number of these images suggest *something* big and frightening," Levy said, "but it wasn't defined." Levy told the children that it was good they had left a mystery in the poem.

Later, several students told Levy they were thinking of a shark.

The genius of Constance Levy's work is the way she probes for tiny details, challenging us to *see* with fresh eyes, choosing just the right words to create surprising word pictures. The poem "Something" seemed a perfect conclusion to the session that used movement to create stories.

Several weeks later, I received a phone call from Karsch. "Guess what!" Her voice was excited. "Last week a dance troupe came to perform. Between the pieces they explained and demonstrated elements of dance. Every time the dancers mentioned levels, directions, tempos, ways and qualities of body movements, my kids beamed. They kept nodding and glancing at me. They knew just what the dancers were talking about. Our movement sessions had really taught them the elements of dance. And listen to this! Included in their program notes was background on a dance piece called "Irregular Fish."

I listened as Karsch read from the program: *"The special qualities of aquatic creatures are explored in an abstract way in this dance. The movement conjures up images of sharks, starfish, and all manner of life in the sea, and the costumes just add the right wriggling, wiffling flavor with their flowing fabrics and luscious colors."*

"Can you believe the coincidence?" Before I could say anything, Karsch said, "I can't wait until next year. I'm going to plan a full-fledged thematic unit on the sea, and I'll ask the science, music, and art teachers to plan it with me."

Interdisciplinary thematic units often grow from the inside out. Exploring underwater life through movement could lead to a study of the ocean, and related pieces of literature and poetry. It is the children's responses, their questions, their enthusiasm, that can take a topic of study to surprising places.

6

Storytelling and Music

Adaptable for Kindergarten Through Grade Six

CARL ORFF METHODOLOGY

Jane Frazee's kindergarten music room in a St. Paul, Minnesota private school was a marvelous space with wide picture windows and cheery yellow and blue walls. In this special room, snare and bongo drums, tambourines, xylophones, glockenspiels, gongs, triangles, cymbals, chimes, wood blocks, and claves were carefully placed in a semicircle on the carpeted floor.

Jane Frazee, one of the world's best-known proponents of the Orff-Schulwerk method of teaching music in the classroom, encourages her students to create tales using original music they compose on the broad range of percussive instruments that composer Carl Orff (1895–1982) designed for music educators. Such instruments are splendid devices on which children can improvise their own music, Orff strongly believed. In addition to using the standard instruments that Orff called his *instrumentarium,* Frazee, and other music specialists who follow Orff's methodology, sometimes encourage students to devise percussion instruments of their own from objects such as tin cans, jars, pieces of metal, cardboard tubing, rocks, sticks, and seeds.

Orff further believed that children must create their own sounds to combine with the percussive instruments: clapping hands; patting thighs; snapping fingers; stomping feet; vocalizing sounds, chants, and songs. Orff's mixture of percussive instruments and body and vocal sounds can produce powerfully original classroom compositions. These pieces are often based on nursery rhymes, poetry, fables, and folk or fairy tales.

ARNOLD LOBEL'S "THE CAMEL DANCES"

The day I visited Frazee, she was using "The Camel Dances," one of Arnold Lobel's *Fables*. I knew the story but had never told it.

"Since my classes are only forty minutes long, I keep the instruments on the floor ready to play so not a minute is wasted," Frazee explained, handing me Lobel's book. "The children will be here in ten minutes, you can learn 'The Camel Dances' by then. It's short." I hurried out to the hall to master the piece (using this book's quick-and-easy method of story learning, of course!).

I concentrate on the camel, who is determined to realize her dream of becoming a ballet dancer. In the story, however, fellow camels scoff at such ambition and continually taunt the striving camel, who perseveres and succeeds. Although Lobel moralizes at the fable's end, "Satisfaction will come to those who please themselves," I do not plan to state the moral as part of my story. Long ago, I discovered that children are natural philosophers. They delight in determining for themselves the often multiple meanings and messages buried in fables and other story genres.

Kindergartners bounce into Frazee's music room and take their places on the rug. I tell "The Camel Dances," using ten precious class minutes.

Frazee asks, "What is the moral of the story?" "Never stop believing in yourself no matter what," Jamie says. The children have much to say about her critics' response to Esmerelda, the name the class assigns to the artistic camel.

"Now that we know the story, we need to think about movements Esmerelda makes as she practices her ballet steps," says Frazee.

Quickly responding, the kindergartners make camel moves: pirouettes (a full turn on one's toe), releves (leaps), and arabesques (standing on one leg, stretching one arm forward, the other arm and leg backward). Working in place, they invent their own camel dances, using ballet steps and turning and leaping in the hot desert sun. Quite often, this exercise borders on silliness because poor Esmerelda is terribly clumsy, and can barely maintain her balance. The class seems to perceive just how hard the camel works to perfect her steps.

"What instrument should best represent the sound of the camel?" Frazee asks. The alto xylophone, for its low tones, because camels are such heavy creatures, the class finally agrees. One boy insists that Esmerelda wear camel bells around her neck for her recital. So bells are added. "I think the glockenspiel should be used when she leaps to suggest how light and airy she feels," Mary volunteers. "Maybe the bass xylophone should be used as she falls," says another student.

Frazee directs the children to sit behind their instruments and create music to reflect Esmerelda's movements. "What other sounds do we need to help tell the story through music?" Frazee asks. Martin says that a gong at the beginning of the story could represent the sunrise. The class wants disagreeable percussion noise as her critics poke fun at Esmerelda. Then, Frazee helps the class create a chant:

> *She is "lumpy and humpy."*
> *She is "baggy and bumpy."*
>
> *Not a dancer. Not a dancer.*
> *Never will be, never was.*

In fifteen minutes, the children are ready to tell the story again, with music, movement, and a chanting chorus of "rude camels" in the audience. A kindergartner and I narrate the story. A little girl plays Esmerelda, the camel who dances—not an easy role since other children who are playing camels taunt her as she dances. But Frazee chooses a well-adjusted child to play Esmerelda, and she has no trouble handling the negative chanters.

Time is up. The kindergartners line up for lunch, pleased with their accomplishments. I stay to talk with Frazee.

"Listening skills are essential in my music room," Frazee says. "I teach the importance of having respect for each other's ideas. These children are just kindergartners, but they already are beginning to understand the relationship between sound, movement, and story."

I ask Frazee whether the children will polish "The Camel Dances" by working on it further. "Not for performance," she says. "Today's lesson was to tell a short fable, add movement, a chant with chorus and instrumentation, and we did that. Tomorrow we will reflect on what we did today. Children have a hard time thinking and talking about what they learned. We will discuss how music not only helped the camel dance, but interpreted the camel's feelings and those of her critics. We may play some of the story again, giving other children a chance to express their musical ideas."

In future classes, Frazee reminds children of their work on "The Camel Dances," recalling with them how they solved nagging composition problems. "I try to help my students 'revisit the elements' of something we have done in the past, calling upon what they have already learned to help them solve other musical problems as they arise. In this way you teach students to continually reflect on what they have done in the past, applying that experience and knowledge to new tasks."

CREATING A SOUND STORY

Developing a sound story, using the whole class, is a lesson in cooperative learning, patience, and flexibility. Everyone contributes at some point and senses story ownership. The resulting story is usually an exciting composite of ideas. Interaction between "story weaver" and children requires cooperation and risk. No one knows how things will turn out; trust is crucial. The story weaver blends student ideas, stimulated by percussive sounds, into the unfolding tale.

It was the last week of school. The temperature that early June day was 90 degrees; the humidity, 95 percent. Amy Beabout's hot and sweaty third graders had just finished recess and were vying for choice places in front of the electric fan. When they had cooled, I asked them to sit on the carpeted floor, which had been cleared of desks so that I could demonstrate the instruments I had laid out on a table:

- hand drum
- tambourine
- slap stick (two pieces of plastic attached to a handle; it produces staccato clicks when slapped)
- claves (resonant wood sticks)
- two-tone wood block
- jingle bells
- large dinner bell
- tiny tinkling bells
- cabasa
- small xylophone

Here is how the story unfolded.

Joe: A Sound Story

I played the cabasa, a Latin shaker with metal beads strung around a metal sheath. Its *skritch-scratch* sound rasped in its sharpness. Julie waved her hand. "Sounds like a man pushing a broom in a street," she said.

"Wonderful! Our main character will be a man pushing a broom in the street," I said.

"What does the man look like?" I asked, playing the cabasa.

"He is poor; he is wearing a rag patch shirt from the Goodwill," contributed Marvin.

I rang the sleigh bells. "Bell bottoms," said Lucy, "His pants are ragged brown bell bottoms." I rang them again. "So when he sweeps the street you can hear his bells?" "That's why they're called bell bottoms," a child called out. Someone else added, "And he's wearing an old white fishing hat."

"Does that mean this down-and-out street sweeper was once a fisherman?" The class nodded. Melissa said, "His name is Joe and he cleans streets in a town in Maine by the seashore."

"Maine?" asked Ronald. I explained, "That's a state north of New York on the Atlantic Ocean. It's where our story takes place. . . . in a small fishing village."

I repeated the raspy cabasa sounds. Robert said, "That's the sound of Joe's broom as he swooshed water and leaves and sticks from a recent storm into a gutter."

I jangled the tambourine.

"Oh! The storm is coming back."

"And there's hail."

"Suddenly Joe is swept into a gutter full of swirling water."

"Towards the storm sewer," called Jeremy. One could feel the tension in the classroom. I inserted some background on the power of flash floods, imploring the class to weigh the seriousness of Joe's predicament. "What happened next?"

Tanya said, "Joe was swept away through the sewer into the ocean." I said, "Yes, that is what happened, but not quite yet. You have to think about how Joe actually *got* to the ocean from the storm sewer."

The children sat quietly thinking. I improvised a slow pattern on the xylophone as the children chime in, adding to the plot. "Yes!" they agreed. Joe was swept to sea from the storm sewer." Someone added, "But a school of dolphins saves Joe by nudging him to the shore of a small island off the Maine shoreline." Someone else called, "He is unconscious. He is suffering from hypothermia."

I said, "Yes, Joe is near death as he lies on the sandy beach." The children are somber. I hit a clicking pattern on a wood block. "What might this sound suggest?" I ask.

Marie said, "Footsteps!"

"Yes," I said, "footsteps. It was a friend of Joe's. Whose footsteps are these and where is this person walking?" The class seemed relieved to find some assistance for poor Joe lying near death on the beach of the offshore island.

"It's a small girl," Margaret volunteered. The class agreed.

"What is her name?" I asked. "Molly." "Mary." Two answers simultaneously. We called her Molly Mary.

"Was she rich or was she poor?" I wondered. Ideas poured out. "She was a poor little rich girl," said one of the third graders, with no dispute from the others. I broke in to explain what that ambiguous phrase might mean.

Molly Mary, the class concurred, lived in a big house on the street that Joe swept every day. Her parents were wealthy, but Molly Mary had no friends except Joe, whom she greeted daily—until the day after the storm, when he failed to appear.

The class continued its exuberant improvising. The children decided that the wood block's *click, click, click* are Molly Mary's footsteps as she runs up the attic stairs of her seaside home to look through her father's powerful telescope. In the gutter below, near the storm sewer, she spots Joe's white fishing hat stuck on debris, then she sights Joe through the telescope lying on the beach of the small offshore island.

There was a pause. I played a *scritch scratch* sound on the cabasa. "A boat! It's Molly Mary and her mother pushing their row boat from the sandy beach out into the water to rescue Joe!" someone said. I rang a bell. "But just then," someone added, "Molly Mary's father, coming in to the habour in his fishing boat, reaches Joe first and brings him safely home." The story had a clear and happy resolution.

I wished there had been more time to work with Beabout and her third graders to learn what happened to Joe, as well as to find out more about dolphins, hypothermia, storm sewers (the kind that swept Joe to sea), and large Victorian seaside mansions. But the summer break was approaching, and these students would have to imagine what else happened to Joe and Molly Mary on their own.

Beabout and I would have to wait until next year to pull out the basketful of Orff instruments and work on fresh sound-story adventures with her new class.

7

Children as Playmakers and Playwrights

Adaptable for Grade One Through Grade Eight

IMPROVISATIONAL PLAYMAKING

The year I assisted Gail Huffman-Joley as a Title I language arts specialist. In her class of family-grouped first through third graders, we had a cluster of children who demonstrated unusual interest in making up plays. It was Huffman-Joley who helped me become aware of the learning taking place during the children's improvisational playmaking sessions. Not only did the children have to collaborate and cooperate, but they were developing oral language skills and putting into practice their budding understanding of the elements of plot.

Although some of the plays were short, others took the children many weeks to perfect before they were ready to share the work before the class. Although none of the scripts were written down, small groups of children involved in a particular play would sometimes write out pages of narrative for scenes, bring props from home, create sets from turned-over desks and chairs, and make costumes from odds and ends of fabric or construction paper.

"These small clusters of children were so determined to produce plays, completely on their own, practicing in the hall during spare moments, there wasn't much we could do to stop them, if we had wished to do so," commented Huffman-Joley, reflecting on this unusual class.

We made positive comments on each presentation, followed by gentle reminders to speak louder or more clearly and to face the audience. Somehow we both sensed the importance and power of children making up their own plays, removed from teacher input.

But not all the children were involved in these productions. Concerned that some students might have felt left out, we invited Ruthilde Kronberg, a storyteller who sometimes uses a method she calls "group puppetry" to involve every child in the class in the playmaking process, into the class.

Group Puppetry: The Power of Role Play to Help Change Negative Behavior Patterns

Following the telling of the story, from which children learn story line, characters, and sequence of events (story bones), Kronberg hands puppets to each child for the retelling of the tale. There is no stage. Instead, Kronberg places chairs in a circle from which child puppeteers speak their parts using their own natural language, not words read from a script. Some scenes that include music or dance are played in the center space.

Kronberg's story this day involves a kindly, gentle princess who is also creative, and a problem solver. When a witch cast spells on forest animals, turning them to stone, stashing them in her cave for some wicked purpose too terrible to contemplate, the indignant princess (an animal lover) is determined to rescue them. But in the process of confronting the witch, the princess herself is captured and thrust into the cave.

Using her wits, and a magic charm given to her by a kindly palace wizard to whom she had gone for advice, the princess pretends to be under the witch's power. When the princess breaks the witch's spell, she and the liberated animals plot their escape, defeating the witch in the process. It is an exciting story, and the children are anxious to play it out.

Kronberg asks for volunteers to play various parts in the story. Lanie raises her hand to play the princess.

Lanie was not an easy student to have in class. She was intense, full of surprises, often acting out frustrations or trying to get attention through her behavior. Frequently she taunted the other children. Once she jumped on my back from the top of a table, grasping her arms around my neck from behind, clasping her legs around my waist like a koala bear clutching a tree trunk. No one knew what Lanie would do next, and many of the children were somewhat frightened of her. She rarely took part in the small groups' playmaking.

Kronberg said, "Of course, Lanie, you may play the princess." I caught looks of surprise from her classmates.

Lanie amazed everyone by playing a sensitive, yet strong and inventive princess, taking no nonsense from the witch. (An unusually quiet child, Annie, played the witch.) Lanie, as princess, demonstrated concern for each of the animals caught under the witch's spell, nurturing and comforting each one as her magic potion transformed the dogs, cats, sheep, birds, and frog statues back to life. This nurturing side of Lanie had not been reflected in her classroom behavior. Annie seemed to enjoy playing the witch role, cackling and casting spells. Both princess and witch roles were chances for these girls to try on roles that demanded a range of feelings and behaviors that were different from their everyday patterns. They could live for a bit in another character's shoes and experience, vicariously, sensing what someone else felt and how they responded to circumstances in their lives.

Lanie never lost her temper and displayed a talent for drama that I had not suspected. For the first time, Lanie got to see herself as a respected member of the class. The other children told her how well she played the princess. The children saw her and she saw herself in a different light—not in the troublemaker role that she had established for herself with her previous behavior in class. Lanie demonstrated to me the importance of encouraging children to try on all sorts of roles during dramatic play.

After our group puppet play was over, children continued to act out the story on their own. They signed up to use the sack of puppets hanging in the closet, not only to reenact Kronberg's "Princess and the Witch," but to create original puppet plays of their own. Lanie entered into this play frequently. She still displayed her temper periodically, but her desire to participate and be accepted helped her modify her own behavior.

Movement and Story Play

No one has helped me more to see the power of exploring the expressive arts to expand creativity, stimulate emotional and intellectual growth, and foster interactive learning than William Freeman. Freeman is a gifted movement therapist and teacher of expressive arts with children, youth, and adults with disabilities, and their nondisabled peers. He developed and directed a program for the Kansas

State Board of Education that has now become an educational organization, Accessible Arts, Inc., in Kansas City.

It took me years of working with Freeman to realize how basic movement is related to the learning process. Once I watched him playing a game called Add a Movement, in which children standing in a circle contribute various movements which they repeat in a rhythmical pattern (see Appendix B). Some shy ones showed their embarrassment by shrugging, or raising their eyebrows when it was their turn to add a movement. To the smallest gesture Freeman responded, "Wonderful! That's a terrific movement." The child would respond, "But I didn't move anything." Freeman then shrugged or blinked his eyes, mirroring the child's movement. "This is what you did. We'll add this movement to the game." And we did. (Freeman always cautioned us not to mimic the child, which would make him or her self-conscious, but to reflect the quality of the movement.)

Catching the smallest physical response someone made helped that person see the importance of the contribution. This affirmation built self-esteem, and for a moment everyone believed, "I can do it!" Freeman called these small physical responses *pulses*. "Find the pulse, respond to it, expand it," he said.

Playmaking with Movement: "Steadfast Tin Soldier"

Watching Freeman work with a group of fourth graders who had been reading Hans Christian Andersen's "Steadfast Tin Soldier," I saw how he listened to the children, and picked up on their ideas before plunging into movement based on the story.

One of the scenes in the story seemed particularly exciting, even frightening, to the children. The steadfast tin soldier has fallen out of a window, ultimately ending up in a paper boat that is swept into a rain gutter, then through the sewer, then out to sea.

Before playing the scene using movement, William established his safety rule: "Be safe to yourself and to everyone else." He reminded the children that when they are moving, it is important for them to be aware of other people moving around them. Then he played music suggesting rain.

Everyone in the work/play space, a cafeteria in the basement of the school, became raindrops falling through the sky. Working in twos and threes the children expressed qualities of water, wind, and clouds. Freeman encouraged the children to change the tempi and intensity of their movements.

With some side coaching, the children now all became steadfast tin soldiers—a challenge because the soldier has only one leg. The hopping around got difficult; children bumped into each other, and some fell down. Quickly, Freeman saw that they had lost concentration and had become self-conscious and silly. Stopping the exercise, without reprimanding them, he suggested that ten children make a boat. How they did it was up to them. The children knelt on the floor, stretched out their arms, and clasped hands. With their bodies they shaped a boat with pointed bow and stern, wide in the middle.

Freeman suggested that one by one other children become waves that gently buffet the boat, using only one body part—a finger, a toe, an elbow. (He had prepared the children for this experience by playing body part awareness movement games at the beginning of the session.) As he directed the children playing the boat to respond to the children playing waves gently brushing against them, the boat began rocking and rolling slightly. Freeman appointed one person to become the tin soldier to stand in the middle of the boat and not fall. There was total concentration.

When the scene was over, we talked about the meaning of the word *steadfast,* and how the tin soldier, even with the handicap of having only one leg, was courageous, able to cope and never give up.

This kind of movement work takes experience and practice, but when children are encouraged to play out what interests them in a story, they work hard to bring the story to life. Improvisation is important to this kind of work; sometimes it works better than other times. The key is to reflect on why the exercise worked, or didn't, make notes, and keep trying.

Playwriting and Classroom Play Production: A Conversation with Kate Kollman

In Kate Kollman's third-grade class I observed another dimension of playmaking that included children performing plays they had written as part of their writing workshop. What was her secret? How did she get third graders to become playwrights and producers of plays?

RUBRIGHT: Children from your class are famous in your district for writing and producing plays. How did playwriting begin in your classroom?

KOLLMAN: I've always believed that dramatics can help students recognize that they are individuals with special talents, and that through role play they can learn to better understand others, but the value of actually writing plays I discovered by accident.

By the middle of my first year of teaching, I knew that more traditional methods of teaching reading and writing were not working for several of my students. My classroom structure already included a daily writer's workshop, but it did not include writing plays. Playwriting began when I realized that one of my students, I'll call him Mark, hated writing, but was a natural storyteller.

RUBRIGHT: Did you ask him to write his story in play form?

KOLLMAN: No, not initially. I began by asking Mark to write down his family stories during writing workshop. My students go through a process of brainstorming what to write about, edit their early drafts, which I call "sloppy copies," then work in small groups to fine-tune final drafts during peer editing sessions. When Mark read his personal experience stories, the children loved his work. He was very funny. But he was embarrassed to let children know how little he had actually written and covered this up by slipping into improvisation, capturing everyone's attention by his antics and humor. Children weren't aware that he was telling the story, not reading the little he had written. But I was.

RUBRIGHT: So you used the personal experience story to help Mark become more comfortable with writing?

KOLLMAN: Yes. Writing was very difficult for him, but at least now he was motivated to try. In fact, Mark was my inspiration for helping other children use personal experience as material for their writing. But I didn't think to ask Mark to write his family stories in play form until I saw how naturally he acted his stories out, and realized that other children wanted to act out Mark's stories too. This was how writing plays became one of the choices children could make as they decided what kind of writing they would do in writer's workshop.

RUBRIGHT: How did playmaking grow from there to include other topics?

KOLLMAN: From that point, interest in playwriting grew naturally. I didn't have much to do with it. When Mark wrote his family story as a play form, other children wanted to read it and play it out. Writing plays became popular. We expanded topics for plays to include stories we had covered in reading, or books that I had read to them, and other subjects that related to other curricular areas.

RUBRIGHT: How did the children make the transition from writing plays to producing them?

KOLLMAN: First, we read plays the children wrote. Acting them out was a natural outgrowth of reading them. Children took turns taking parts in one another's plays. Soon they were memorizing lines and going out in the hall to practice. From this point the children made simple props and costumes from construction paper or brought things they needed from home. They took their productions very seriously, but I didn't do much, except give them time to develop and practice their work.

RUBRIGHT: I am interested in the fact that the children memorized the lines. Didn't memorizing lines cause undue stress for some children?

KOLLMAN: I was amazed to find that the children loved memorizing lines. In fact, many children got great pleasure from memorizing the entire play. If a child forgot a line, the other children knew what it was and cued the person who forgot. I now realize how sad it is that teachers almost never ask children to memorize anything except basic math facts and some rules of grammar, punctuation, or spelling. I would never have dreamed of making children memorize lines to a play. They did it all on their own and derived great pleasure from doing so.

RUBRIGHT: What about plays that are already written for children to read or perform? Did you use these plays in addition to plays your children wrote themselves?

KOLLMAN: Absolutely. I realized that not all children enjoy writing plays, but it seemed that all the children enjoyed reading them. I searched for published plays appropriate to third-grade reading level that would also enrich every part of our curriculum. Soon plays on all kinds of topics became important to every aspect of my teaching.

RUBRIGHT: Can you give an example?

KOLLMAN: I once found a play on endangered species that fit into my science and social studies curricula. Each child had a copy. When the children realized that plays are written to be performed, they wanted to perform everything. Of course, there was not time to perform every play. We decided which ones we could devote special time to. The children divided the parts according to who wanted to be in the play, memorized lines, and put the play on. There were no auditions. Children took turns playing certain roles.

RUBRIGHT: Were all the children involved in playmaking?

KOLLMAN: Yes, in one way or another. All the children read plays in reading circles—either the children's published plays or commercially published plays. But children were involved in different ways when a play was in production. Not all children are comfortable performing, so some chose to build simple sets or make props. Some preferred to direct or produce.

RUBRIGHT: You did not see yourself in the role of director or producer?

KOLLMAN: Never. The plays were primarily child-written, then produced and directed by them. I helped children edit, revise, and polish their plays during writer's workshop as the pieces were prepared for "publication." It is during the writing process that children learn about grammar, punctuation, spelling—what I call *mechanics* of writing. Publishing our own writing is a very important part of writer's workshop. Publishing plays became another kind of writing the children could do.

I videotaped the production so children could study their work. The videos helped the children discern whether they spoke loudly enough, whether the movement was natural and appropriate to the character. They critiqued their own work.

The plays were produced by the children. I was facilitator and helped manage time so that all our time was not spent on play production, seeing to it that other curricular needs were met daily.

RUBRIGHT: Did the plays the children produced have props and costumes?

KOLLMAN: Yes. But some plays were simple. If the children were doing a play on food groups to go with our health unit on nutrition, they made paper vegetables to pin on their clothes. Or masks. We did most of the art in our classroom. I was a beginning teacher when I started doing plays as part of my curriculum, and didn't feel comfortable asking the art or music teacher to help.

Looking back, I see that they would have been willing. Nevertheless, I like doing all aspects of the play production in my classroom. I could be sure the plays integrated with our other studies, and could keep the plays simple and eliminate the danger of the plays becoming big productions where product was more important than process.

RUBRIGHT: Do you have a background in theater, or creative drama?

KOLLMAN: Very little. In elementary school, I was involved in a few class plays, but only performed in one major play in high school.

RUBRIGHT: But no drama courses as part of your teacher education training?

KOLLMAN: Nothing was offered in creative drama, improvisation, movement, or storytelling. These topics were only touched on in my undergraduate elementary education language arts courses. Actually it was my mother, a master teacher, who mentored me in several areas, including drama. Primarily, I stumbled onto the power of creative drama by accident when I realized that my traditional teaching style was just not reaching some of my children.

RUBRIGHT: If you had a background in creative drama, I wonder if you would have discovered the effectiveness of playwriting and having children memorizing lines—rather than children using their own natural language.

KOLLMAN: I don't know. I just found that the children really enjoyed memorizing lines of both plays we did—both child-written and those commercially published.

I discovered that many of my most talented actors were children who were just not doing well in academic subjects. Some of these children were from disadvantaged backgrounds. They had trouble learning math facts and rules of grammar taught in traditional ways, but they memorized lyrics of songs and lines for the plays in no time. Not only were these children verbally expressive, they showed such acting talent. Their success in our classroom plays helped their self-esteem enormously. In traditional subjects they were doing poorly; in playmaking they were excelling.

RUBRIGHT: Since discovering the power of using drama in your classroom, have you taken additional courses to further develop your interest in this area?

KOLLMAN: I plan to do this. Teachers need much more training in how to determine children's various learning styles. I have discovered that drama, writing plays, and playmaking are some ways to do this.

RUBRIGHT: Based on your experience, do you think teacher training programs should include teaching the expressive arts as part of their training?

KOLLMAN: Absolutely. Courses in creative drama and storytelling should be made mandatory in every teacher certification program. Unfortunately, when the funds get tight, programs in music and art are the first to be cut. These arts, as well as drama, are as basic to learning as any other subjects we teach. But I had to discover this on the job; I was not taught how to integrate the arts, especially drama, in my teacher training program. I had to learn this on my own.

RUBRIGHT: What about the other teachers in your building? Did their children create plays, too?

KOLLMAN: Not generally. One year a class of fifth graders collaborated with my third graders and produced two plays (each group contained half fifth and half third graders). They worked together in the hall practicing and making sets, costumes, and props. Then the two groups shared their plays with each other. It was exciting.

RUBRIGHT: If playmaking is so motivational, as a means for integrating reading and writing and creative expression, why do you think more teachers don't try it, at least once in a while?

KOLLMAN: There are many reasons. Perhaps lack of confidence in knowing how to begin is a factor. Remember, I stumbled onto playwriting and playmaking accidentally, out of a great desire to help some of my reluctant writers. Also, some teachers may hesitate to try playmaking out of a concern for the amount of time it takes.

I must continually balance my curricula to be sure I spend sufficient time on basic content that I am required to teach. By integrating the curricula, however, I solve many of these problems. With a little planning, I can connect math, science, social studies, language arts, and art with playwriting and playmaking.

I experimented with something that I thought might help children like Mark, a natural storyteller, and it worked. Now, I can't imagine teaching without playwriting and playmaking as part of my everyday classroom experience.

8

Learning Tales to Tell—
Quick and Easy
Listening and Reading

Adaptable for All Grades

When teachers include storytelling among their teaching strategies, they discover how the art form benefits students by helping them:

- recall and retell story sequences by visualizing not memorizing text
- understand components of plot
- expand their understanding of story genres, topics, and themes
- hone critical and analytical thinking skills
- apply tools of effective telling using eye contact, oral expression, gesture, and movement
- expand appreciation of cultural differences that stories reflect
- discover the reasons for reading
- improve reading skills
- develop positive self concept

One of the easiest ways to learn a story to tell is to repeat one that has just been heard. Even first graders can learn tales to tell by using such a method.

Another method is to learn stories by initially reading and rereading them from the printed word.

Over the years I have devised a nine-step process for quick learning of material to tell from text: picture books, short folk- and fairytales, fables, short pieces from literature, segments of biography, or bits of history, lore, or legend.

QUICK AND EASY METHOD TO LEARN A TALE TO TELL FROM TEXT

The following method is adaptable for students grade 3 through adult (also see Chapter 15).

Goal:

Each student learns a tale to tell alone to the class.

Objective:

Pairs of students learn a tale to tell from a written source before sharing them solo.

Step One:

Each pair receives a short fable or folktale.

Step Two:

One student reads the story; the partner listens, eyes closed.

Step Three:

Switch; the other partner reads while the first reader listens, eyes shut.

Step Four:

Partners discuss the story's bones: setting, characters, sequence of events (incidents), conflict, crisis, resolution.

Step Five:

Without looking at the printed page, visualizing the tale in their minds' eyes, partners take turns telling short segments of the piece round robin until it is completed. Using natural language, they do not memorize the story word for word. In this key step, students are encouraged to muddle through the tale visualizing in sequence what happened, when, where, and why.

Step Six:

Partners fine-tune their story by discussing it again and determining what factors might improve its rendering, such as sound effects, more characterization, facial expressions, and gestures.

Step Seven:

Partners separate, each finding a place in the room to "tell the tale to the wall." Since all storytellers in the classroom tell to the wall simultaneously, no one should be self-conscious or embarrassed. In this step, tellers try to get through the story by themselves.

Step Eight:

Storytellers find new partners, then tell tales to each other (making sure each pair has different tales to tell).

Step Nine:

After practicing and polishing their stories, storytellers present their pieces to the class as part of the class's "storytelling festival."

There are many variants of this basic structure, such as: small groups of students working together to tell a story collaboratively, using a format that often includes role playing, music, and movement. Productions that come from group work lead to "story theater" performances. (Exercises in Appendix B help students fine-tune skills for this process.)

On the other hand, some students prefer to learn stories on their own by immersing themselves in the story, rereading it many times to clearly master its bones (basic components of plot). Again, the objective is not to memorize word for word, but for the teller to visualize the details of the story, telling what is seen in the imagination.

As students develop stories independently, peer coaching—when classmates make notes on each other's telling—can help to perfect the tale, sometimes using a checklist that includes:

- eye contact
- flow of language
- clarity of vocal expression
- smoothness of telling the tale, including how well the storyteller engaged the listeners, bringing them into the story
- gestures or movement
- characterization

These quick-and-easy methods of learning stories from text are nearly foolproof when applied to most students third grade and older, but they need adjusting with children who are poor readers.

One fifth-grade teacher, Pat Vogl, with three markedly poor readers in her class, made sure that their partners were good readers. First, the good readers read the story to their partners, who were poor readers (Step Two). The poor readers, who now knew the story line, read the tale back with minimal stumbling. This boosted their self-confidence immeasurably.

During the time her students were polishing their stories to tell, Vogl offered the following additional suggestions:

- Jot down your ideas for developing characters and embellishing plot details, especially where conflict or crisis occurs. (Vogl's students kept storytelling journals for purposes of documenting stories they were collecting and learning.)
- Tell your story to parents, siblings, friends, in front of a mirror, or to the cat until it "rolls smooth off the tongue."

Vogl helped her students see further possibilities for rendering their tales well by studying the styles of professional storytellers recorded on audio- and videotape. Her students also played drama and movement games to experience ways in which their stories might be enhanced through movement and music (see Appendix B).

Although students could learn a short story to tell using a quick-and-easy method in an hour, they discovered it took longer to polish the tale for a more formal presentation.

Once the practice sessions were completed in Vogl's classroom, the students were ready for a storytelling tour of the school building. Mini-storytelling festivals became popular in each of the classrooms visited.

Vogl found that some of her students who had poor reading and writing skills displayed an amazing talent for storytelling. Their renderings were more freely expressive than those of some more academically able children.

Teachers often remind me that students who are not doing well in school frequently respond to storytelling. These children often exhibit an intense interest in listening to stories, and demonstrate surprising talents to tell tales. Such revelations underline the importance of providing more opportunities in classrooms for alternative ways of learning, and for abandoning, when necessary, traditional teaching methods that do not engage students in the learning process.

A TEACHER TELLS "THE SUN AND THE WIND"

During a practice telling session, Vogl told me of an experience that she had when her class insisted that she also tell a story.

"Impulsively, I sat in the storytelling seat and told 'The Sun and the Wind,' a fable I remembered from our literature book, but certainly had never thought of telling. Perhaps I was inspired by my children, but suddenly I found myself spontaneously adding gesture and characterization.

"You should have seen me dramatizing the Sun, who was determined to win his bet with Wind as to which was most powerful. As Wind, I gusted and blew; as Sun I became hotter and hotter. It seemed that neither would win, until Sun said, 'See that man walking down the road? Whichever of us can force him to take off his cloak wins the bet.' Wind blew harder, but the man only held his cloak tighter around his shoulders. But Sun shone, warmer and warmer, and soon the man removed his cloak. Sun won the bet!"

"But Pat," I said, "you must have told lots of stories during your years of teaching. Why was telling 'The Sun and the Wind' different?"

"Oh, sure," she replied, "but just stories about my kids and the dogs. My dog stories are great for getting children to tell and write stories about their pets. But I never told a 'real' story like *'The Sun and the Wind'*." (See Chapter 15 for a version of "Sun and Wind" to tell.)

"Stories about your family and pets *are* real stories," I responded. "In fact, stories about personal experiences are perhaps the most important stories we can tell. They force children to reflect on their own lives and become material for writing and telling autobiographical stories."

"I guess my dog stories could develop into a storytelling unit with an animal theme," responded Vogl.

"Why not?" I answered. "You already ask your class to write pet stories. After telling their pet stories, you could ask them to study animal behavior and habitat. Soon you'll have an interdisciplinary storytelling unit that bridges language arts with social studies and science."

We all know that teachers often exercise the most natural form of storytelling, relaying anecdotes from their own lives. When teachers tell about themselves—the things they know best and love, and personal experiences that have been meaningful to them—I have observed that children grow quiet, listen intently. When children focus on such stories told by their teacher, I know that, consciously or not, that teacher is in "story mode."

Teachers are in "story mode" when their audience is engrossed in an anecdote, personal recollection, joke, or folktale delivered by the teacher. Such informal storytelling can occur throughout the day, no matter what subject is being studied.

Often, and quite mistakenly, teachers sense that storytelling requires a formal telling of a carefully prepared story for a specific purpose. I remind them that telling carefully prepared stories is only one aspect of storytelling. Storytelling is the way we communicate, mirrored in ways we listen, deliberate, and interact. Stories in all their permutations enrich and fill our language.

As an example of how storytelling techniques can fit into the curriculum, I recall a sixth-grade language arts class that I once taught. "Take out your dictionaries," I requested of them, "and find a strange or unusual word. Just be sure you know what it means, how to pronounce it, and why it would be a good one for us to learn." Soon we were listing the words on the board.

Next, we played with the words and put them into phrases, sentences, paragraphs. Working in pairs, children improvised stories with strange settings and bizarre characters. In effect, the class was doing fantasy writing. Then, we added dialogue, introduced conflict, added a crisis, and finally resolved the situation. By the end of the period, we had completed a dictionary-vocabulary-spelling-grammar lesson that supported a mix of thinking, speaking, and creative writing skills.

"I do similar things," Vogl responded. "I just never thought of such activities as storytelling." Upon reflection we agreed that effective teaching means being a good communicator, and good communication often relies on storytelling to dynamically underscore vital elements of instruction.

THE POWER OF STORYTELLING TO REACH, TOUCH, AND TEACH

Vogl's zest for storytelling deepened. She decided that her class should tackle the Norse myth *Beowulf.* "*Beowulf*!" snorted her lunchroom colleagues. "Yes," she said, "with creative drama extensions in the gym!" As the project unrolled, I assisted it in my role as the storyteller-in-residence. Initially, we gave students copies of Rosemary Sutcliff's book *The Dragon Slayer,* a version of the *Beowulf* saga, and asked that the class read the book thoughtfully.

Vogl and I told several episodes from *Beowulf* to stimulate interest in the story and to encourage students who were having trouble with the reading to stick with it. Simultaneously, Vogl initiated lessons on the influence of North Sea ocean currents on weather, Scandinavian geography, and historic settings for *Beowulf.*

Timmie, a student with serious social problems, was totally absorbed in the *Beowulf* project, particularly its writing component. For the first time in months, he was given the author's chair in front of the classroom to share his own *Beowulf* writings. His peers listened respectfully as Timmie read a long paper on the meaning of a struggle between Beowulf and Grendel. It was an astonishing perspective from a bright, sensitive, troubled fifth grader, and perhaps gave an insight into his own feelings of being misunderstood in the classroom.

Once, in the midst of a storytelling unit in a fourth-grade class, Johnny, a new boy, had transferred into the room. Johnny asked me if he could join the class storytelling team, which was scheduled to tour other schools. I explained that the other children had been practicing for a month. "But I've already got a story I could tell," he begged.

With some hesitation I took him into the hall, where he recited his story, an expressive version of "Wicked John and the Devil." The previous day, a guest storyteller had performed it for the class; Johnny had memorized it almost word for word from hearing it told once.

"Great job, Johnny," I said, "You may join the team tour, if it's okay with your teacher."

The teacher told me that she was willing to give Johnny a chance, but since he had a record of serious behavior problems, the principal was reluctant to let him go on tour.

"Johnny's been no problem during our practice sessions," I said in the boy's defense. "He listens intently to the other tellers, he's patient, and is very constructive in suggestions or notes he gives to other tellers. Why not give a child who has trouble elsewhere in his school life a chance to shine where he functions well?" As a result, Johnny toured, demonstrated his talent, and was not at all disruptive.

After the tour several months elapsed before I revisited Johnny's classroom. I knew that Award Day was on the horizon and suggested to his teacher that we give ribbons to the storytelling team for their hard work. "Terrific!" she said. I prepared Olympic-style blue ribbons.

The principal questioned our proposal to reward Johnny with a medal since he had accumulated a record of harassing other children on the school playground.

I insisted that Johnny deserved a ribbon for his role as a storytelling team member, and I won the argument. At the ceremony, Johnny proudly walked amidst 350 children and teachers in the auditorium to receive his ribbon. His peers viewed Johnny in a new light, and he saw himself rewarded for a talent he had worked assiduously to develop. To cap off Award Day, a group of parents was so impressed by Johnny's potential that they funded a scholarship to send him to a summer creative drama camp at a nearby university.

Whether learning from an oral source or learning a tale from a text, students who tell stories as part of their everyday school experience are learning many communication and interpersonal skills. They are also delving deeply into content that may not otherwise have been of interest to them. Students of all abilities seem to enjoy stories and storytelling, but often it is those who are not responding to traditional teaching methods who seem to benefit the most.

THE COPYRIGHT ISSUE

Students can choose material to tell from many literary genres: fables, folktales, fairy tales, lore, myths, legends, sagas, and history, finding as many versions of a story as possible to deepen appreciation and understanding of the cultural roots from which the story came. Although individual versions of the tale may be copyrighted, the basic story content of folkloric and historical material is in the public domain. The more this material is studied from a variety of sources, the more storytellers can craft their own versions.

Literary tales are original stories created and copyrighted by an author. Written permission to tell these stories must be obtained by writing the publisher, who may charge a royalty fee to use the material.

Copyrighted material cannot be audio- or videotaped without additional permission, and, possibly, royalty fees. To avoid problems with copyrighted material, I encourage storytellers to tell material from the public domain or craft their own stories from their personal experiences.

9

Ananse the Spider
Storytelling African Style

Adaptable for Grades Three Through Eight

Ananse the spider is a trickster folk hero of the Ashanti tribe in Ghana, West Africa. When the Ashanti came to the Western Hemisphere, most as slaves, the Ananse tales came with them. Today many people of Ashanti heritage living in Central America, the Caribbean Islands, South America, and African-Americans in the Southern United States still tell Ananse tales.

What's the appeal of the Ananse tales? It's Ananse's basic, and convoluted, character, which alternately represents jealousy, greed, gluttony, trickery, foolishness, honesty, deviousness, and sometimes, wisdom. Children infer that Ananse's complex personality reflects the range of behaviors possible in human experience. Even young children can spot recurring moral issues presented through the tales, especially fair play versus cheating or serving oneself as opposed to recognizing the needs and wants of others. When Ananse plays tricks that get him in trouble, children think it is only fair that he is embarrassed and/or punished as a result of his outrageous behavior.

MULTICULTURAL STORYTELLING: ANANSE'S DANCE

When Dr. Ben Halm, a Ghanian performer, playwright, and scholar, visited my university undergraduate language arts class to demonstrate the participatory style of African storytelling, he asked my students to sit on the floor. Improvising a hypnotic, repetitive beat on his drum, he directed us to clap to the rhythm. Several students picked up instruments—claves, shakers, tambourines—to add their own percussive patterns to Halm's beat.

Halm jumps up and whirls around the room. Swirling, swooping, reaching up, he pantomimes Ananse's mother-in-law, who is digging and planting rice seeds. Gouging out the make-believe earth with his hand, dropping in seed, stomping the earth into place, his dancing body yields to the basic beat and improvised syncopated rhythms.

Then come the sounds. Halm's voice crescendos in a joyous trilling of the tongue. He utters soft shouts. He beseeches students who are sitting wide-eyed in their places to "Come join the dance!" Most look away, embarrassed, hesitant.

Halm leaps, twirls, shouts. "I was there! This is what I saw!" he cries as he chants part of the tale. "Were you there, too?" No one responds.

I fear that the momentum will slow, that a remarkable opportunity to participate in a storytelling experience led by an African artist will be lost. If my students' inhibitions aren't overcome, our session will revert to a lecture-demonstration, a mere discussion of this vibrant folk art. Halm needs the class's response *now*.

So, I jump in. "I was there! I saw it, too!" I shout, joining Halm in the dance, adding my voice to the jangle of sounds.

"What did you see?" Halm shouts. I respond, "Ananse sneaking a hatful of his mother-in-law's delicious hot bean stew to eat in secret." "What do *you* see?" Halm asks a student. "I see Ananse pressing the hatful of hot beans onto his head, when his mother-in-law sees him," she answers.

"Look! Ananse is dancing a new dance! A hat-shaking dance!" says Halm, acting as Ananse gyrating in pain as the bean stew burns his scalp under his hat. "Look at Ananse's new dance," I shout, playing a villager who comes to find out what the commotion is about. "Teach it to us, Ananse. Teach us the new dance."

My students catch on. First one, then another jumps up. They ignite into movement. My students swirl through the room, losing inhibitions while they mirror Halm's Ananse dance. Halm now softens the intensity of the movement; soon he barely moves to the basic beat, STEP, step, step; STEP, step, step. Now only the clapping rhythm is left. The rest of us fall to the floor, exhausted.

Halm brings the story to an end. "Ananse," he says, "can no longer endure the pain of hot beans on his head, so he removes his hat, bean stew dripping down his face. And his head? It has been burned bald. The villagers laugh. Embarrassed, Ananse runs to hide in the tall river grasses where he pats cool river mud onto his skull. And that is the reason, to this day, that spiders have bald heads, and hide when they are embarrassed in the cool tall grasses." (See Chapter 15, "Ananse's Dance.")

We feel pleased that we have participated in an authentic Ashanti storytelling experience.

"You didn't experience authentic Ashanti storytelling," says Halm. We are surprised. "But you are African; you are a storyteller from Ghana," we reply.

"No matter," says Halm. "There is no way I can tell Ananse stories 'authentically' because my heritage is not Ashanti. But I can treat the material with respect and play with the stories improvisationally in the African idiom."

"African storytelling is very improvisational," Halm continues. "As we gather around the fire at night, someone begins to sing. Stories are told through song, then danced, just like what you did by playing Ananse dancing with a hat of hot beans on his head. Of course, there are people who are very, very good at the art form. But in Africa someone from the audience might jump in, yelling, 'I see it, I was there!', adding whatever he wants to the story until someone else enters and takes over the story."

As do fables, Ananse tales teach lessons. "Ananse's Dance" playfully demonstrates how trickery, gluttony, and shielding the truth led to unfortunate consequences—Ananse's eternal baldness.

Halm knew that my undergraduate students were developing an interdisciplinary, multicultural storytelling unit using Ananse the Spider stories. They were doing this to initiate a study of the Ashanti people of Ghana for their respective elementary classrooms.

Halm cautioned, "It is impossible to really gain a true appreciation of another culture unless you immerse yourself in it over time. This includes visiting the country."

Halm reminded us how difficult it is for people to transcend their own ethnocentricity. He agreed that we were correct in studying a people by reading or telling their folk- or fairy tales. He told us how stories can help us discover similarities between peoples the world over, despite differences in dress, food, rituals, beliefs, geography, political structure, and economics.

Inspired by Halm, my students were ready to learn their own Ananse tales. Using a quick-and-easy method of learning a story, they worked in small groups. Several class sessions later, each group presented their Ananse tales. "I never told a story in all my years growing up, nor do I recall hearing stories told in school," one student confessed to me. "Now I can't imagine teaching without telling stories."

ANANSE THE SPIDER STORYTELLING UNIT

My undergraduates discovered that the Ashanti are noted for music, dance, and artistry in weaving and textile designs. Kente cloth—narrow strips of gold, red, blue, and black silk blends traditionally woven by male weavers—is worn toga-style by royalty. Today Ashanti fabrics and designs are recognized the world over for their beauty.

As they studied, the class learned that central to the Ashanti oral tradition is the legend of the Golden Stool, which, it is believed, descended from above onto the knees of Ashanti Chief Osei Tutu to signify his leadership over a federation of chiefdoms. The Golden Stool became a sacred symbol of the Ashanti nation.

According to one legend, the original sacred Golden Stool may have been melted to pay war debts in the late 1700s. Today, the Ashanti chief's sacred stool is made of wood, covered with gold, and used only during official royal ceremonies. The Sacred Stool has its own chair which is brought out for special occasions; this stool must never touch the ground.

Each chief commissions a new stool to be designed and carved for him during his reign. When the chief dies, the stool is blackened and put in a special place in which the spirit of the chief is said to reside.

My students found that the Ashanti value proverbs, such as:

"He who cannot dance will say the drum is bad."
"Around a flowering tree one finds many insects."
"What is bad luck for one is good luck for another."
"To make preparations does not spoil the trip."

They were excited to connect how similar the lessons of the proverbs were to those embedded in the Ananse tales.

Halm's visit helped us appreciate improvisational storytelling, African style. He also reminded us how the Ananse tales should lead to a study of a culture's beliefs, customs, and values, respecting the historical and cultural framework from which they came. (See Chapter 15 for Ananse Tales to Tell.)

10

Family Folklore
Storytelling and Creative Writing

Adaptable for All Grade Levels

For children in all grade levels, a family folklore unit can be a rich learning experience. Interviewing friends and relatives; studying old photographs; reading diaries and journals; and researching stories of heirlooms help students chronicle their family histories.

Topics for a Family Folklore Storytelling Unit include:

- Adages, sayings that reflect moral values, wisdom, and philosophies of family members
- Diaries, journals, letters
- Embarrassing moments
- Emigrant tales and other stories of moving or relocation
- Everyday rituals and chores
- Family heroes and heroines
- Family heirlooms
- Fortunes lost and found
- Holidays, birthdays, family traditions, special events
- Humorous events
- Milestones: courtships, weddings, births, funerals
- Pet and animal stories
- Photographs (who were these people, when and where?)
- Transportation: horses, wagons, carriages, buggies, boats, trains, automobiles, planes
- Trips and travel adventures
- Turning Points

Researching family stories develops listening, thinking, speaking, writing, reading, and researching skills. For example, reading Cynthia Rylant's picture book *When I Was Young in the Mountains,* which highlights Rylant's family remembrances, can trigger similar memories in teachers and students. These memories can be shared orally as part of the family folklore unit, then written and illustrated in class-produced books or albums.

Inviting parents, elders, and professional storytellers to class further stimulates interest in the topic. Parents and grandparents are often unaware of how important stories of milestones, turning points, and family traditions are to their offspring—until they begin sharing their memories.

Although student ethnic and religious backgrounds may differ, the sharing of personal stories allows students to discover similarities between people, while learning to respect and appreciate their differences. Such sharing also serves as raw material for original tales that children can write, polish, and illustrate as historical fiction. (See Appendix A: Designing an Interdisciplinary Family Folklore Storytelling Unit for cross-curricular possibilities.)

ELDERS SHARE THEIR STORIES

When Georgene Brunner, a guest elder, shared memories of her young years with June Von Weise's third graders, I realized how charmingly personal values shined through her stories. Brunner displayed treasures she had brought: her grandmother's amber candy dish, a small doll bed that was a gift from her grandfather, and samples of her brother's early efforts at embroidery. "Yes, my brother embroidered this cat on this tea towel," she said. "And, in seventh grade he knitted a purse for his teacher. There's nothing wrong with a boy trying his hand at embroidery and knitting.

"I was loved and treated well as a child," she said, "but I was expected to do what I was told. I mowed the lawn with a hand mower, washed and ironed, but I never learned to cook. When I got married I was worried. My mother said, 'If you can read, you can cook.'

"But I can tell you that I didn't get everything I wanted. If I said I wanted something, my mother said, 'You don't need it,' and that was that. One time I remember seeing President Franklin D. Roosevelt and his wife, Eleanor, in Vincennes, Indiana. There were little souvenir umbrellas being sold. I wanted one so much I thought

I would die. My daddy said, 'You don't need that.' I didn't get one, and you can see that I didn't die."

Maggie raised her hand. "I know a story about a little girl who wanted a pony so badly that she told her parents, 'If I don't get that pony, I'll die.' And that night she died. And her mother said, 'Oh, if we only had her back, I'd buy her one hundred ponies. But it's too late.' "

Von Weise asked Maggie where she had heard that story. "It's a story poem from my favorite book, *A Light in the Attic* " (Silverstein), she replied. "The poem says that if you want something very much, tell the story to your mom and dad to let them know you might die, too, if they don't get you what you want . . . (pause) . . . but that's like a joke, get it?" Everybody laughed.

Brunner concluded with a story about singing her first solo for a church Christmas program when she was five years old. She sang another at her college recital. Both times her eyes searched the audience for her mother and father to give her confidence. "You know, I believe that things you learn to love right now will somehow be important to you all your life. I became a music teacher and taught in this very school until I retired!

"Already, you are building your memory treasures," Brunner continued. "I wish I had kept a journal like you are doing when I was in third grade. Think of all the things I could tell you!"

"BAKED POTATOES"

Since Von Weise wanted the children to listen to more family stories, she invited me to return and tell some of mine. I came the following week and told "Baked Potatoes," a story I wrote based on material told to me by an elderly friend, and on my own experiences growing up in Chicago. I explained that "Baked Potatoes" is historical fiction.

Baked Potatoes

The sun from the window shone on the strands of gray hair that had dropped from the bun tucked at the nape of Miss Celia's neck. She sat in a rocker; a wool lap robe lay over her frail legs. I asked, "Can you tell me about something special you liked to do when you were young?"

"Well," she said, "one thing I liked to do was go skating on the creek in Kirkwood Park. But you know," she paused, reflecting, "my mother never let us kids go skating until the potatoes were done baking.

"My father was a salesman. He took the train from St. Louis to Chicago to get new products he would sell door to door when he got home. Every day, my sister, Margaret, my brother, Paul, and I would listen for his footsteps on the porch. When Papa finally returned, he placed his heavy black valise on the front room floor. When he unlatched the brass locks, the suitcase fell open. We peered inside at Papa's new line of goods—usually just dishtowels, teas, coffees, spices. But nestled deep inside we knew there were 'pretties' for us —mostly sticks of gum and penny candy. But always there were the soaps: little bars of soap from hotels where Daddy stayed in Chicago.

"Each of us got a few to add to our collection. I kept mine in a box under my bed and on rainy days, I'd call, 'Who wants to trade soaps!' Then Paul, Margaret, and I would sit on the front room floor trading our piles of brightly sheathed little soaps back and forth the way children today do baseball cards.

"One time when Daddy came home and opened his valise, we peered inside to see three pairs of shiny black leather shoe ice skates with gleaming silver blades. At first, we thought skates were his new goods to sell door to door. Then he pulled out the biggest pair and gave them to Paul. Next, he gave a pair to Margaret; the smallest pair he gave to me. We could hardly wait to go skating on the creek in Kirkwood Park!

"But, you know, it was the warmest winter St. Louis had had in 25 years. Every day we rushed downstairs, out onto the porch to check the temperature, but it wasn't until after Christmas that we had a cold snap.

"After a week of near zero weather, my mother said at supper one night, 'Edmund, why not walk down to the park to see if the ice on the creek is hard and safe for the children to go skating in the morning.'

"That night there was no arguing about who was going to wash, dry, and put away the dishes. We tucked ourselves into bed without fussing. Lying awake, we waited for Papa's return. When he finally came into each of our rooms, he knelt by our beds for prayers, then whispered, 'The ice is hard and safe. You children can go skating in the morning.'

"We were up at the crack of dawn, pulling on long underwear, hand-knit wool socks, sweaters, scarves, gloves, and hats. We threw our skates, unlaced and tied together, over our shoulders, and marched downstairs. Paul led, followed by Margaret, then me. After a quick breakfast of toast and hot chocolate, we made for the kitchen door. 'Wait a minute,' said Mother. 'You're not going skating until the potatoes are done baking.' You didn't ask my mother 'Why?'

"Bundled up, we stood by the kitchen door. Finally, Mother pulled six hot baked potatoes from the oven and put them on the kitchen table. We watched her wrap each one in a square of brown paper. Stuffing a baked potato into the toe of each skate, she said, 'Now, children, by the time you walk to the park, your feet will be cold, but your skates will be warm.

"Slipping and sliding on the wheel ruts frozen over with rain water in our dirt road, we teased and laughed our way to the park, where we sat on the cold rock ledge near the creek to put on our skates. When we unlaced our shoes and slipped our cold feet into our skates, we discovered those hot baked potatoes had been keeping our skates warm! Paul said, 'Stuff the potatoes into your shoes while we skate.'

"We skated and skated until once again we were chilled to the bone and our toes were numb. When we took off our skates, we found those hot potatoes had kept our shoes warm! 'Stick the potatoes in your pocket,' said Paul. Since they were no longer warm I wondered why, but you didn't argue with my brother.

"Walking home we were too cold to laugh and tease. Paul strode ahead. With my short legs I tried to keep up with Margaret. Suddenly, I noticed Paul had pulled a cold potato out of his pocket. 'Margaret,' I cried, 'look at Paul! He's eating one of those cold shriveled potatoes.'

"Margaret didn't say anything, but pulled a cold potato out of her pocket and ate it. Well, it was a long walk home. And I was hungry. I pulled a cold, shriveled, baked potato from my pocket, peeled back the brown paper, and took a bite. Nothing has ever tasted so delicious. Imagine a cold baked potato without salt, butter, or gravy tasting so good."

Miss Celia adjusted the lap robe draped over her knees. "You know," she said, thoughtfully, tucking escaped wisps of hair into her bun, "I liked to skate on the creek in Kirkwood Park when I was young. But telling this story has made me realize that what I liked best was eating cold baked potatoes walking home."

Discussion

Von Weise and the children talked about the story.

"What was in the suitcase?" Von Weise asked. She listed on the board the items children named: ice skates, soaps, coffees, and teas. "What else might have been in the suitcase?" Children brainstormed other objects that could have been sold door to door, as well as "pretties" that could have been surprises for the children.

"If you had a father who traveled and who always brought you a gift when he returned, what might you dream of getting?" She began a second column on the board called "Wishes."

Von Weise discussed expectations of things hoped for but yet unseen; she wrote the word *anticipation* on the board. This led to a discussion of hope.

"Why is hope such a good thing to have? What's so wonderful about hope?" she asked.

The children thought about it. Aisha said, "Hope is like a wish that things will get better or change."

Von Weise sighed. "There isn't a day that goes by that I don't *hope* someone in class will understand math a little better."

"What made the skates such a wonderful gift?" she asked. "They were unexpected," said Melanie.

"But there was disappointment, too," said Von Weise. "Remember there was no ice because it wasn't cold enough. And when there *was* ice, the children had to wait at the door for the potatoes to bake," she said.

"They had to have patience," said Mark.

Von Weise nodded; she guided the discussion elsewhere. "The potatoes kept the skates warm for the children's cold feet, but what else can cause us to feel warm?" she asked.

Children chimed in. "Food." "Clothes." "Fires." "Somebody caring for you." "Good deeds." "Things you do for people." "Love." Von Weise wrote these on the board. All these are ideas that you might use as you write your own family stories.

I told another story about a favorite holiday, Thanksgiving. Once a year, the story unfolded, Grandma, Grandpa, aunts, uncles, and children squeezed shoulder to shoulder around the dining room table.

After the feast, the women took leftovers into the kitchen and the men retired to the front room to smoke cigars and pipes. The children slipped under the dining room table, pretending no one knew where they were hiding.

This story led to a discussion of holiday celebrations, feasts, favorite foods, and secret hiding places. Von Weise and I worked with the students individually as they discussed versions of family stories that they were writing. Von Weise continued to help her students edit and revise their stories, and the children often shared their works-in-progress with one another for ideas and suggestions. Returning two weeks later, I listened to the children read their finished pieces.

CREATIVE WRITING: CHILDREN'S FAMILY STORIES

Kelly's story is based on an experience her mother had as a child.

Beads in Noses

Once when my mom was just a little girl, about five years old, her mom was working in a Catholic hospital. When she quit they gave her a little turquoise sewing box with really tiny beads around the edges. One time she took the box and went under the table (the tablecloth was all the way down to the ground so no one could see her).

After she got under the table she picked six beads off the box. She was so excited because she just learned how to count. She stuck the six beads up her nose three in each nostril. Then she got out from under the table and went to tell her mom. She was so excited that she learned how to count. Her mom called her dad at a church meeting. She told him to get home right away because they had to take my mom to the hospital. The doctors had to go up in her nose and it *hurt*. She still has a bead in her nose to this very day.

Rachael's story is about a birthday.

Valentine Birthday

Ding Dong. I knew it was either Sue and Doug (my godparents) or one of my grandparents at the door. They were coming to celebrate my birthday. I ran to the door! It was my godparents. As soon as they were in they sat down on our couch. Then Ding Dong! My grandpa and grandma were there. Then Grandma P. came in and sat down. She sat on the couch too. That was the nearest piece of furniture to the window.

After all of them arrived, my mom came from the kitchen. Dad came from the basement. Sarah came from upstairs. After that the "Hi's" and "How are You's" began. Then Mom went into the kitchen to finish the icing on my cake. When Mom told me to ask everyone what they wanted to drink I knew dinner was soon. We were having ham, brocili and rice. I was the birthday girl so I got to pick what was for dinner!

When we got settled down Mom gave me the "It's Your Day Plate!" Anytime you do something really special you get that plate! Today was my birthday so I got the plate.

Doug (my godfather) took our picture. He loves to take pictures. Sue (my godmother) was making a funny face. We had to take it over again.

After dinner we all went to the living room and talked!! We talked for almost half an hour or longer. My Grandma P. was so funny. She kept telling wonderful jokes. I think everybody was happy. Then Mom told me it was time to unwrap presents! I yelled, "Yippie." But it was Valentines Day so everybody got presents. Even though I got to open one first. The only present I remember getting was a small teddy bear.

Finally, it is time to blow out the candles. Whooosh! I blew them all out!! "Yippie." I said. "Rachael, I didn't get your picture," said Doug. So Mom lit the candles again. I took a deep breath and "Whoosh!" Well, I didn't get them all that time, but Doug said it would be a wonderful picture. So I happily blew out the rest of the candles. Next, I got to cut the cake. I cut 3 small pieces for my grandparents, 4 semi-large pieces for my parents and godparents and 2 large pieces for my sister and me.

When I asked her how she helps her third-grade children write so well, Von Weise said, "It isn't always easy. Learning to give meaningful criticism which helps children perceive their own errors is a delicate business. If they become discouraged they may learn to dread or even hate writing. And I am not always successful maintaining everyone's enthusiasm for writing. Some children have trouble finding their own writing style, their own 'voice.'

"I told Jenna that I am looking for something special in her writing style that will help me recognize her work even if her name is not on the paper," Von Weise says. "She is writing about taking piano lessons. I told her that when I was her age I memorized the music during my lessons instead of reading the notes. My teacher discovered I was memorizing the notes because I needed glasses and couldn't see the music. When I said, 'Jenna, tell me something about your piano lessons that only you can express because only you lived it,' she wrote a revision of 'My Piano Teacher.'"

My Piano Teacher

My piano teacher is nice. I started taking piano in 1993. I never liked to practice piano but my mom made me. My piano teacher's name is Mrs. H. Every time I practice 30 minutes I get to get something out of her shopping drawer. She has a Grand piano. Her house is big, it is a 2 storey house. The piano is in the living room. I can remember my first recital. I was so nervous. I was playing O come All Ye Faithful. There was a huge crowd. I was so nervous I messed up on the first note I played. After the recital was over we had punch and cookies. The next time I went to piano lessons she gave me a statue of Bach.

Von Weise complimented Jenna on her piece. "It really sounds like something only you could write. You are beginning to find your voice."

Later Von Weise told me, "When the sixth-grade teacher shows me a piece of quality writing by one of my former third-grade students, I know the writing the children did when they were my third graders helped bring them to where they are today. I also realize the importance of daily writing in all subject areas. But it isn't always easy to keep students interested in the writing process. That's why the family folklore concept is so useful. When older guests come to share their stories, we continually find new things to talk and write about."

ALICE JACKSON'S CLASSROOM VISIT

I suggested we invite Alice Jackson, an amazing seventy-eight-year-old friend who has been coping with the loss of her vision for the past ten years, to be interviewed by the children. Von Weise was enthusiastic. "Wonderful! We have been reading inspirational stories about people who have disabilities, including blindness. I'll tell the children you are bringing a special elderly friend, but I won't tell them that Alice is blind."

A week later, I guided Alice Jackson between clusters of desks in Mrs. Von Weise's classroom. The third graders quickly sensed that our storytelling guest was blind.

"Just place my hand on the back of the chair," Alice said, as we neared the front of the room, "then I can feel where to sit, and sense where the children are when I speak."

"Alice lost her sight ten years ago," I said. My introduction included a story about Alice learning to fly a small plane when she had her vision. "Once she landed her small plane in a snowy cornfield when she lost sight of the landmarks on the ground that guided her to the landing field, " I added. "Now that she has lost her vision, Alice has taken up ballroom dancing." I held up a mint green chiffon, sequined, feathered dancing dress, and a pair of silver shoes we had brought to show the children.

Alice said that in dance competitions she wears dresses like the one we brought to class. "I do one hundred sit-ups every day to keep in shape. My partner is over six feet tall and my arms get tired reaching his shoulders. I lift barbells to strengthen my muscles. My dancing partner leads me so well that some people don't know I am blind." I held up medals Alice had won in competition.

"Tell the children about the time you went up in a hot air balloon, Alice," I said.

"I wanted to do a free fall from a plane with a parachute to cele- brate my seventieth birthday," she replied, "but my daughter wouldn't let me. She said, 'Mother, you're blind! How would you know when you were ready to land, and what if you got hung up on a tree or landed in water?' So she made me take a balloon ride. It was nice, but *so* tame. Right now, I'm waiting for the weather to get better so I can go riding on my friend's white motorcycle. I don't think I'll tell my daughter until after I've done it."

"Do you have a seeing-eye dog?" a student asked. "No, I don't, but my daughter raises horses in the country. I told her, 'Diane, do you think you could train one to be a seeing-eye horse?' So far she hasn't.

"But I do have a cane." Alice pulled out a white cane folded into twelve-inch sections held together with elastic cord. "Look!" She pulled the elastic; the pieces snapped together into a cane. "Do that again," the children pleaded.

Alice told the class that she doesn't use the cane in her house because she knows by heart where all her furniture is placed. "I call the empty spaces, between the furniture, my walking path," she explained.

"Once my granddaughter, Rachel, left her toys on my walking path, and I fell over them. Rachel was so upset that I might have hurt myself, she strung a clothesline over the TV and chairs to remind her to keep it clear of toys."

More questions. "How do you know what time it is?" Alice pulled back her sleeve and pressed a button on her wristwatch. A voice said, "Ten-twenty." "My watch talks to me," said Alice. "In the morning it also serves as an alarm clock. My son-in-law programmed this watch to wake me up at six-thirty each morning and it rings like a rooster. But I don't know how to turn it off. It crows twenty times before it stops! Sometimes I hate that rooster crowing."

"How do you know what's on your plate to eat?" a student asked. "The people at the Society for the Blind told me to think of my plate as a clock. When someone tells me, 'Alice, your meat loaf is at twelve o'clock, your peas are at three o'clock, your potatoes are at seven o'clock,' I know just where everything is. Sometimes I make a mess when food falls off the fork. But I've learned how to eat without many accidents."

"What about your clothes? How do you know what you're wearing?" asked Susan. "I don't always," Alice said. "The woman who helps me during the day puts my clothes in the drawer a certain way, so I memorize where my underwear and pajamas are. But I can't see colors and sometimes I make mistakes. Do my colors match today?" Alice's crisp, curly white hair contrasts with the bright red of her dress and her black jacket. The children assured her everything matched.

"One day I went dancing wearing two left shoes. They were the same color, so nobody noticed until I wondered aloud why my feet were hurting. One of my friends said, 'Alice, you're wearing two left shoes.' At least they were the same color." She laughed. "The most important thing I have learned to do since becoming blind is to laugh at myself."

Alice explained that sometimes she performs as a clown named Gardenia, using a puppet to demonstrate problems blind people have and give tips on preserving one's sight.

Alice apologized for having to leave early. She had a dancing lesson.

ALICE STORIES

After she left, Von Weise asked her students to jot down ideas that came to them as they listened to Alice. Later, the students were encouraged to use their notes to write stories about Alice.

Walking Path

by Ashonda

This is not the brick road in the Wizard of Oz where Dorothy, the Scarecrow, the Tin Man, and the Lion skipped down the path looking for the Emerald City. This is Grandma Alice's walking path. She has a rope going around chairs and tables. It starts in her living room leads to the dining room next to the kitchen and to her bedroom.

Alice has a granddaughter named Rachel. Years ago Alice told Rachel not to leave her toys in the path because Alice would fall. One day Rachel did the thing her Grandma told her not to do. Grandma was walking through her path but she did not fall because she went through her dining room. The toys were on the bedroom path.

Many blind people came to visit Alice and walked on her walking path.

Alice makes *all* people she knows feel happy in her own special way.

Alice's Talking Watch

by Jenna

Alice's watch said, "It's 10:38." When Alice needs to know the time she pushes a button on her watch. Alice is a busy person. She needs to know the time when she has organ lessons or dance lessons. Alice needs to know what time it is to be a clown. Her clown name is Gardenia. When Alice goes balloon riding she needs to know when to go up and when to come back down. And when she is going to see (the movie) "Grumpy Old Men," she needs to know what time it starts and what time it is finished.

When Alice is going to church she needs to know what time it is. And when she is going to meet someone she needs to know the time. When Alice does not know when to wake up, a voice on her alarm clock, that sounds like a rooster, crows 20 times. Alice is watching for the time a man on a white motorcycle will carry her away. Do you know why Alice needs a talking watch? Because she is blind.

Wake Up!

by Joey

Alice Jackson gets awakened every morning by her rooster alarm clock. I think it would be annoying being awakened even if your alarm clock didn't blow its batteries at 6:00 AM cock-a-doodle ooing at you! and I would especially hate it doing that 20 times every morning. I would get very bothered if it only made a ruckus one time every morning. But even if the alarm clock is bothersome in the morning, the talking watch she wears during the day is a big help to blind people like Alice Jackson at other times. Like if she had an appointment at 10 AM and she pushed her watch button and it said, "It is 9:42 AM," she would know to hurry and get to wherever her appointment is.

Exercising

by Yolanda

Alice Jackson does 100 sit ups everyday. She has a lot of energy. It's hard for me to do that much. She is 78 years old. I can't do that much. She loves doing that. One day I want her to come to gym class so she can give me all the energy and strength that she has.

Seeing Eye Horse

by Kelly

The thing I like about Alice Jackson is that she comes up with a lot of good ideas. Since most people have seeing eye dogs when they're blind she wanted a seeing eye horse. On a Monday Alice went to a farm to find a horse for herself. When she got there it was really noisy. The dogs were barking, the chickens were squawking, the turkeys were walking around going gobble gobble, the ducks were quacking and the cats were crabbing at the farmer's wife. A lot of stuff was going on.

When she found the farmer they went to the horse stalls. The farmer told her about each horse and she found the one she wanted. The farmer said he would come to deliver the horse. When Alice got home she thought of a name for her horse and went to buy stuff for it. Alice named her horse Cow-Boy. It was a fine horse.

It was a soft smooth brown horse with a black silky mane. Alice bought a nice leather black saddle and reins for the horse.

By the time Alice got home she didn't see the farmer at the door delivering the horse. The farmer yelled out, "Are you sure you want a horse instead of a dog? I have some fine dogs." "Well, I want to have a horse because it's my choice, O.K.?" said Alice. And the farmer said, "O.K., it's fine with me. Just when that horse ruins your house, don't come running back to me." "Oh, I won't," said Alice.

Two Left Feet: Alice Jackson's Story

by Kris

Even though Alice Jackson is blind she still enjoys dancing.

Mrs. Jackson told us that she once went dancing wearing two left dancing shoes. She was dancing and having fun when a fellow dancer asked her why she was wearing two left shoes. She probably felt embarrassed. I went home and tried squeezing my right foot into a left shoe. Take it from me it's not very comfortable. It would hurt my feet trying to do a turn in two left shoes. It probably felt fine to Alice Jackson because she's a whole lot different than me. I'm not half as adventurous as she is. She's probably very brave to take all the pain and agony into taking one step with two left shoes.

During the students' daily writing workshop, these stories had gone through many drafts, peer editings, and conferencing sessions with Von Weise. Only after the third draft does Von Weise help the children with grammar, spelling, and sentence structure. The children sent an audiotape of their "Alice" stories to Mrs. Jackson, along with three fragrant gardenias, to thank her for coming to their class.

11

History Telling
An Oral History Project

Adaptable for Grades Four Through Eight

MERAMEC HIGHLANDS

When Michael, Harry, and Sam charged into her fourth- and fifth-grade classroom and dumped fragments of pottery, plates, cups, and a bent spoon on her desk as she took milk count, Mrs. Handley looked up and saw three boys bursting to tell their story. "Maybe you boys should tell us what this is all about," she said.

"We found a ghost town with an abandoned railroad station and a tunnel where the train went through," the boys excitedly told their classmates.

Michael held up the plate. "My mother said the houses in our neighborhood were once cottages that were part of a big summer resort called Meramec Highlands before the main lodge and dining hall burned in the 1920s. This plate might have been what someone ate from back then."

"How can we learn more about this ghost town?" asked Handley.

"Maybe we could find people who lived back then who could tell us the story," said Marianne.

"Maybe we should all go on a dig," Handley said.

Puzzled, the children looked at her. Then John said, "You mean like archaeologists do when they hunt for buried treasure?"

"Exactly," said Handley.

That is how the Meramec Highlands project began. When Handley, the children, and several parents went on a dig at the Kirkwood, Missouri site, a local TV news team tagged along to document the event. Artifacts were brought back into the classroom, cleaned, and placed on a table. "What do we do now, Mrs. Handley?" asked Suzanne, eyeing the collection of shards.

"What do you think we should do?" Handley responded.

A discussion followed. "Do you think anybody is still living who remembers going there?" asked Derek.

"How do you think we might find out?" Handley asked.

Someone replied, "Maybe we could run an ad in the local paper."

"Not a bad idea," said Handley. "But let's start by telling Mr. Loudenslager [the principal] about the ghost town you found."

Loudenslager referred Handley's students to Mrs. Billie Fogerty, a history buff who lived on Meramec Highlands property. The project was off and running. Tracy Leiwicke, a specialist in collecting oral histories, taught the children always to ask, "Who else could give us more information about this?" When the children asked Fogerty this question they learned about several elder citizens who became instrumental in helping them gather the information they needed.

"Kids acquired such independence during this project," Handley said. "They had no fear of looking up phone numbers of people, calling, making appointments for an interview. Of course, they had to have parents' permission.

"Children never dreamed that our older citizens would be so interested in talking with them. Real friendships developed between the students and elders. One woman invited the children to her farm. When another favorite senior entered the classroom one day, the children gave her a standing ovation.

"So much information was gathered that we formed committees to sort and edit it. Organizing and writing this material became a common class goal. Everyone wanted their book sections to be exactly right—interesting information and no misspelled words."

Handley arranged for historian Katharine Corbett from the Missouri Historical Society to train the students in how to conduct interviews for oral histories. Corbett told the children:

- Be sure there are fresh batteries in your tape recorder.
- Test to be sure the machine is recording.
- Always have interviewee provide name, address, and phone number.
- Ask open-ended questions, not questions with simple yes or no answers. Be sure the interviewee knows the topic on which you want information.

• Ask interviewees to sign simple release forms that state their quotations can be used for the purpose you have in mind.

Corbett told the children it was important to think about what they want to learn and to prepare questions that will lead to this information prior to the interview. She said finding the person who had information they wanted was not always easy. Corbett demonstrated the process by interviewing an elderly guest who knew about Meramec Highlands.

Then the children volunteered to go into the field to interview and tape elderly volunteers on the resource list Fogerty had prepared for them. If they didn't own one, children borrowed tape recorders from the school. Parents drove the children to the various elders' homes and waited in the car while the students gathered information. "What could these kids be talking about for an hour?" wondered some parents. When parent volunteers began transcribing the tapes, they found out.

FINAL PRODUCT: THE KIRKWOOD BOOK

Raw material from the tapes, edited by committees of children, was slowly evolving into a book. Photos to illustrate the book were contributed by elders and other Kirkwood citizens.

Handley kept me posted on the oral history project. "We have had bake sales to help supplement what the PTO and school district contributed to cover the cost of printing the text," she told me. I attended the party at which students presented autographed copies of their coauthored book to the senior guests who had contributed stories and photos.

Several children read excerpts from their book, *Kirkwood As It Was (1895–1929): Meramec Highlands.*

Meramec Highlands, a luxurious summer resort with a hotel, cottages, and spa, opened on May 5, 1895. There the people could enjoy a variety of facilities, from row boats to a general department store. Meramec Highlands also had a large ice house packed with 70 tons of ice. In addition, there were a dairy, deer lodge, spring house, company stables, wagons, steam laundry and livery stable.

Meramec Highlands included 438 acres and cost over half million dollars for buildings, water works, streets, sewers, electric light plant.

The Highlands became so popular that the Frisco Railroad began running trains out on a regular basis. It was a forty minute ride from Union Station (downtown St. Louis), costing ten cents. A ticket for one hundred rides cost fourteen dollars and seventy-five cents. During the height of Meramec Highlands' popularity, three hundred to five hundred people passed through the train station daily.

The hotel was one of the most elegant hotels in the country at this time. It had five floors and one hundred twenty-five rooms. The conveniences were outstanding for the times, but under today's standards, it wouldn't even pass inspection. The Highlands had no indoor plumbing, but it had running water which was considered a great convenience.

Royalty came from all over the world to enjoy the health spa. There were about twenty-four baths, and each held forty gallons of water. Each bath also held 40 oz. of minerals from the springs. The water contained eleven different minerals:

Aluminum sulfate, magnesium iodide, magnesium chloride, lithium chloride, sodium chloride, sodium silicate, sodium bicarbonate, sodium sulfate, potassium sulfate, calcium sulfate, strontium sulfate.

Rates for both hotel and cabins were $15 to $17.50 a week.

The Highlands amusement park had slides, sandboxes, swings, horses, steam merry-go-rounds, scenic railroads, and bicycles for the afternoon. One of the most popular features of the Highlands were the dances called "hops."

Most of the music was jazz. Dances included the Charleston, the Bunny Hop, Tango, Camel Walk and Fox trot. Each dance lasted two and a half minutes and cost a nickel. The owners of the dance pavilions made $900 a day.

Down at the river front people found a variety of recreational facilities. There were fifty rowboats, hourly trips on the steam yacht "Columbia," swimming, and many excursion boats which cruised as far as the Mississippi. Costumes could be rented for "costume bathing." A stone boat house, a store, Mexican burros, even a photographer were added attractions which contributed to the popularity of this exciting summer resort.

The Highlands Inn had a very short life: 1895–1910. From 1910–1929 it was totally abandoned except for a caretaker. In 1929, the

Highlands Inn burned to the ground. The surrounding cabins, with names such as Fairview, Elmwood, Laurel, Edgewood or Ferndale, were sold as conventional homes. Today all seventeen cabins have been remodeled. But some people still think of the cabins as Meramec Highlands.

The elders were impressed, and applauded the effort that went into writing the book. I was amazed when Handley told the guests that most of the work on the book had been done after school. Children made their own appointments. Parents drove them to interviews after school or on weekends. Although children met in committees at school weekly to read, confer with the teacher, revise, and edit what they had written, most of the writing was done at home. They pressured each other to meet deadlines they had set.

THE WRITING PROCESS: A REFLECTION

Several years later, I revisited the project with Leslie Handley. "What we did then," she said, "was process writing, peer editing, and cooperative learning—teaching concepts that were rarely used and had not yet been articulated as effective teaching tools.

"You know," she said, "I tried doing similar oral history units several times with other classes. Wonderful, touching stories always surfaced, but it was never quite the same. I guess it was because the Meramec Highlands project came from the children. It was truly theirs. They worked unbelievable hours after school on it. Today, I stress to teachers the value of this experience. 'Just do it,' I tell them. The stories that evolve from oral history projects are rich and authentic and the young writers are active participants in preserving them."

When she left classroom teaching, Leslie Handley became director of the Gateway Writing Project in St. Louis. "My belief in preserving family histories, traditions, and finding family stories has grown even stronger. In fact, I am now involved in several oral history programs that help elders preserve family experiences and stories. We have a project where elders come into classrooms and exchange stories with the children, who write them down into their own stories and books. For me, an unexpected outcome of this kind of experience is dissolving stereotypes young children and older citizens have of each other. Our project leads to mutual trust and respect."

I knew she was right. Observing June Von Weise's third graders listen to elders tell their stories as the basis of her family folklore/ creative writing unit, I saw that many of the preconceived notions children and elders may have of each other vanished because of the sharing sessions.

12

Eldertel
Senior Citizens and Children
Share Stories

Appropriate for Grades Four Through Eight

Marilyn Probe, a community educator and designer of senior citizen programs, brainstormed alternate ways to stimulate interaction between older and younger people. With a small grant, she designed Eldertel to bring together seniors from urban community centers and children from nearby St. Louis public schools. Working with interested teachers, she invited professional storytellers to serve as catalysts to help children and elders become acquainted, and to begin sharing stories from their lives.

Seniors and children also honed basic literacy skills by writing and reading to each other. Probe hoped that intergenerational experiences in the arts of storytelling, creative drama, movement, music, and puppetry would also help build participants' self-esteem.

MAKING CONNECTIONS THROUGH SONG
AND DANCE

Since the seniors weren't acquainted with the children from the local school who had come to participate in Eldertel at the senior neighborhood center during initial sessions, there was a problem getting young and old to feel comfortable with each other in a short period of time. (Each session lasted about two hours.) Much depended on the ability of the guest storyteller to involve older adults and children in some participatory activity.

When Gladys Coggswell, an African-American singer and story-teller, performed for fifth graders and senior citizens during an Eldertel program, I watched her masterfully trigger interaction between the generations, dissolving mistrust and shyness. When she beat the tambourine and sang "In That Great Day Gettin' Up Morning," old and young joined in, dancing around the room. Soon the room buzzed with conversations between young and old.

When Coggswell asked, "Who used to dance when they were young?", several elders told about jitterbugging and doing the Charleston.

Nonie, a woman in her fifties who accompanied her elderly mother to the program, said, "When I was seven years old, I was paralyzed and the doctor said I wouldn't be able to walk again. And look at me. With the help of my mother, I not only walked but I became a model and a professional dancer. What you children need to know is that you can *achieve* anything with the help of your parents, your friends, and your teacher."

As Coggswell yielded the floor to Nonie, the session took on the flavor of a revival.

"Repeat after me," Nonie said. "*I can achieve anything with the help of a parent, my teachers, and my friends.* Say it loud." The children hollered back. "Say it again, louder." The children chanted the phrase again.

"Good! Now, if you children want to learn the Charleston, I'll teach you." The fifth-grade girls volunteered and Nonie instructed them in the basic steps. Then she said, "Okay, boys, it's your turn. You line up in front of the girls. I'm going to teach you a soft shoe. You ever hear of a soft shoe?" Silence. "I didn't think so." The boys mirrored Nonie as she demonstrated the soft shoe. Coggswell joined in by keeping the beat on her tambourine.

The teacher who had brought the children closed the session. He reminded the elders how important it is for them to pass on stories, skills, and values to the younger generation.

I remember Handley's saying that one major outcome of her students' Meramec Highlands oral history project was that it broke down stereotypes that children and the elderly have of one another. Coggswell showed us that another way to battle preconceived notions is through song and movement.

GROUP PUPPETRY

During another Eldertel session, storyteller Ruthilde Kronberg invited children and elders to participate in a group puppet play. As she synopsized her version of an old folktale, "The Man Who Tried to Change His Luck," Kronberg handed out puppet characters to children and elders who sat on chairs in a semicircle. (See Chapter 15 for a version of this story.)

"Now you know the story bones—the setting, the characters, what happens in the story, and the ending. And you have your puppet characters," said Kronberg. "Use your own words when it's your puppet's turn to speak. Don't worry if you forget what happens next, as I will play the narrator." The puppeteers caught on.

In full view of the audience, the children and elders held the puppets in front of them as they played the story. The child who manipulated the foolish man puppet marched through an imaginary wood where he met the wise woman, the wolf, the maiden, the tree, and finally, God, all represented by elders and children wearing puppets on their hands. Kronberg's narration kept the action flowing.

As they played the story again, the puppeteers became more confident: vocal expression improved; language became more improvisational.

"When I do group puppet plays in the classroom, I include everyone by adding groups of ants, bees, birds, and other animals to the story, often as chanting or singing choruses. Everyone gets a puppet and a part," said Kronberg. "After telling the story twice, the puppeteers do not need me at all. They embellish the story on their own."

Since Kronberg's group puppetry technique is not dependent on a script, poor readers do not need to struggle with text. They are able to play the story as soon as they hear the tale told. Writing and reading activities can build on the initial oral experience. Reluctant students are often motivated to write an original version of the story or invent a sequel. Such literary successes help these students develop a more positive attitude toward learning.

"Although Eldertel is interested in helping older adults and children develop literacy skills, my purpose for group puppet plays is to form a bond between children and elders using folktales from the oral tradition," said Kronberg.

Kronberg, raised in Germany in the 1930s, said, "Eldertel is attempting to capture what has been largely lost in America. In many other cultures generations are not separated; all ages work and play together. Eldertel is an example of how this ancient intergenerational tradition can be revived in America."

Through Eldertel, lines of communication opened between young and old. At ease with each other, children and elders swapped stories from their lives. Some encounters even led to friendships that were followed by letter writing and telephone visits.

(Eldertel is funded by the Regional Arts Commission of St. Louis, the St. Louis Public School Partnership, the Missouri Performing Traditions, the Missouri Humanities Council, and the Missouri Alliance for Arts Education. Eldertel has since been expanded to include Eldermove, hiring guest dancers as artists-in-residence in addition to storytellers for interactive programming.)

13

Storytelling and the Writing-Reading Process
An Interview with June Von Weise

Approaches Adaptable for Grades One Through Eight

June Von Weise's family folklore unit, Leslie Handley's history telling project, and Marilyn Probe's inner-city Eldertel program all involved students and adults telling, writing, and reading their stories.

Strongly interested in the writing process, Von Weise viewed the family folklore unit as another way to help her third graders find interesting subjects about which to write. I asked Von Weise about her methods.

THE WRITING PROCESS

RUBRIGHT: Why *do* your students write so well?

VON WEISE: Writing is a process that helps children learn; it results in finished products. Through writing, students organize their thinking; they share what they have to say. I help the children realize that when they compose text, their process is similar to artists when they create pictures. Each sentence is carefully crafted to communicate with an audience.

RUBRIGHT: Prints of Picasso's *Mother and Child,* Henry Tanner's *The Banjo Player,* and a picture of a Henry Moore sculpture hang on your classroom wall. Is this art a factor in writing exercises?

VON WEISE: Absolutely. We study them for mood, theme, and design. The children make up original stories about characters and settings in the art. We study how the artists compose their work by drawing our eyes toward what they want us to see. We can do this with our writing by emphasizing what we want our audience to notice about characters and settings. How we put our writing together is our composition.

RUBRIGHT: But the subject matter of each painting reflects a family situation. Did studying these pictures and writing about them help prepare the children for the family folklore unit?

VON WEISE: It wasn't until the folklore unit began that I realized that the writing we had done based on the paintings was analyzing relationships in families. Children made up who was doing what, when, where, and why, based on characters in the painting they chose. It was a perfect preparation for the family folklore unit, but it wasn't planned.

RUBRIGHT: You say that it is essential for children to make meaning of their world. Does writing help do this?

VON WEISE: I think so. The children were touched by Alice Jackson's courage and determination. They had to think about how difficult it must be to be blind. Thinking and writing about real-life situations is one way that children make meaning of their world.

RUBRIGHT: When and how do you teach the basics of writing?

VON WEISE: Although the children write daily in each subject area, we work on special writing projects, such as the stories that came from the family folklore unit, from 10:00 to 11:45 two mornings a week.

We have group lessons focusing on punctuation, grammar, spelling, and vocabulary, but mainly the children learn to write by writing, writing, writing. Consistent practice is the key to developing good writing skills. I also work with each child at the beginning of a new project to help them establish good writing habits.

RUBRIGHT: What do you mean "good writing habits"?

VON WEISE: I want children to continually think about the writing process and ask themselves questions that will help them develop a deeper understanding of how their word choices reflect their purpose for writing: What am I saying? Who is the audience for this story? Will my audience know what I am saying? Will my audience understand my way of presenting my thoughts? Is my subject worth the reader's time? With my writing, can I change the way someone thinks? This leads to children discovering their individual style, which begins to help them develop their own "voice."

RUBRIGHT: How do you help children discover their own voice?

VON WEISE: It is hard for children to understand what this means. I encourage them to ask themselves: Have I chosen the best vocabulary and phrases to set the mood of my piece? Does my audience know who wrote this, even if I don't sign my name? Is the piece "me"? These questions help children find a writing voice.

RUBRIGHT: Do you have a favorite method for motivating students to *want* to write?

VON WEISE: Storytelling provides marvelous motivation for writing. The enthusiasm of storytellers we invite to class makes an immediate impact on children. Description, characters, and components of plot are more refined in the children's oral and written work as a result of listening and responding to storyteller presentations. When children see themselves as storytellers, their writing becomes fresher.

RUBRIGHT: Do your children actually *tell* their stories, as well as read their works in progress?

VON WEISE: Yes. I encourage them to tell their developing stories to one another, adding drama and sound effects to their oral expression. When they revise their written versions, the stories reflect the energy, action, and drama of stories they have told, or acted out for one another.

RUBRIGHT: Have you noticed children who have benefited from the storytelling improvisations you do as prewriting exercises?

VON WEISE: Many children benefit in special ways, but Dana's attitude toward learning changed completely due to storytelling.

Dana attends special reading classes to improve her reading skills, but she hadn't shown much interest in reading or writing until we did improvisational storytelling in class. In fact, she sometimes demonstrated her frustration with school through a belligerent and antisocial attitude. Having been kept back a year may have contributed to her lack of self-confidence.

After participating in the storytelling games, Dana's world changed. She immediately made up and told her own stories. And what telling! She had perfect control of vocabulary, motivation of her characters, their traits, plot, and closure. This showed me that she understands story elements. Her surprising talent to render a story and enthrall her audience continues to amaze me.

RUBRIGHT: Has storytelling helped Dana improve her writing and reading skills, too?

VON WEISE: Dana is often easily discouraged as she struggles to express herself on paper, but she was determined to write her story. After a great deal of revising, we went to the computer.

As Dana read me the story, I typed her words into the computer. It was important for her to see that when the words appeared on the screen, they were her words.

RUBRIGHT: This process takes time. How do you justify spending so much time with one student, when the rest of the class is waiting?

VON WEISE: I sensed the teachable moment for Dana had come. She was open, excited, willing to work hard to get her story on paper. It was the first time that Dana had shown an interest in writing. I had no choice but to spend extra time with her *right then.* Other children seemed to understand and worked on their own until Dana and I were finished.

To this point, Dana had experienced nothing but failure in school. She repeated first grade. Her reading and writing skills were poor. Many reading strategies were tried, but nothing worked. Frustrated, she saw no purpose in learning. But the storytelling experience turned her around.

My hope is that by reminding her of the moment when she was able to tell her story and write it down, she will be encouraged to try again and again. I want her to continue to re-capture the feeling of success that hard work produced. When she believes, "I *can* do it," that is when her self-confidence will grow.

It is very difficult to deeply affect a child's negative self-concept. But when they see their work is respected by their peers, children begin to perceive themselves more positively.

RUBRIGHT: How has Dana demonstrated this growth in self-confidence?

VON WEISE: Dana continues to write and act out new stories for storytelling presentations in other classrooms. Her daily journal entries reflect great improvement in writing skills. Dana's attitude toward school has also improved.

She has gone on to learn to tell a Harriet Tubman story which she worked on with her special reading teacher.

RUBRIGHT: Did her reading teacher use storytelling to motivate Dana before?

VON WEISE: No. But the reading teacher now realizes that storytelling is the way to reach Dana—and perhaps other students who are having trouble learning to read in traditional ways.

RUBRIGHT: This brings up the question of learning styles. Is it difficult to infer what a child's learning style is?

VON WEISE: Many children have a variety of learning styles (auditory, visual, kinesthetic), and teachers try to find out what they are through various kinds of testing, but even then it is not easy to find the right approach for each learner.

RUBRIGHT: What did storytelling help you discover about Dana's learning style?

VON WEISE: Dana is an example of a child who has a bodily kinesthetic learning style. I now know that she learns through movement and the kinds of mental imaging that storytelling stimulates. Storytelling seems to reach students who have a hard time learning in more traditional ways. It involves the whole child—the imagination, inventive thinking, creative oral responses, physical participation through movement, role play, and drama.

Before the storytelling experience, I didn't know how to reach Dana. Her tremendous creative energy, imagination, and verbal skills have now been channeled into something through which she can be successful.

RUBRIGHT: Is it true that when Dana discovered that she could make up stories, she wanted to write them down as well?

VON WEISE: This is what happened. She wanted to write her stories so badly that she was willing to endure the arduous process of writing, revision, and editing to get it like she wanted it. When children discover that, through persistence, something they create is received positively by an audience, their work is validated. And their self-esteem rises.

LITERATURE RESPONSE JOURNALS

RUBRIGHT: What kinds of journal writing do your children do?

VON WEISE: The children keep several journals in their desks to use daily in different subject areas, such as math, social studies/science, and creative writing. None are more important than the entries they make in their literature response journals.

RUBRIGHT: What is a literature response journal?

VON WEISE: Through them, children are helped to understand quality literature by writing responses to various aspects of the piece they are studying. They reflect on and analyze setting, characters and their goals, and how rich language creates exciting situations in the text. They come to understand what makes great writing and how to apply techniques of good writing to their own work.

RUBRIGHT: What goes into a literature response journal?

VON WEISE: The children respond to the literature in a number of ways:

- rewriting scenes from a different character's point of view
- making connections to other things they have read on similar themes
- writing letters and poems related to the story text
- inventing dialogues between characters in the story
- creating plays from favorite episodes in the book
- describing their feelings regarding the latest happening in the story
- summarizing the story text they had read to date
- analyzing sentence structure to help understand an author's style and to learn more about how parts of speech work together to create meaning

When the children see how authors do this, it helps them understand the concept of composition.

LITERATURE CIRCLES

RUBRIGHT: How do you structure the reading of literature in your classroom?

VON WEISE: Some books I read to the whole class. But the children also choose books to read in their literature circles. After giving book talks on four choices to pique their interest, I have the children choose the book they want to read. I put children into heterogeneous groups of five, mixing them according to gender, race, and ability.

RUBRIGHT: How does Dana respond in her literature circle?

VON WEISE: At the beginning of the year, Dana wasn't interested in participating. Her reading skills were so poor that she was reluctant to read aloud. She wrote almost nothing in her journal. She wanted acceptance, but she didn't feel that she could find it in our literature circle.

It wasn't until her remarkable storytelling success that she began to make connections between the literature we studied and the reading-writing process. Now, when I suggest activities such as writing a scene for a play or telling part of the story from another point of view, she shares her work with confidence in the literature circle. The storytelling experiences taught her how to do it.

RUBRIGHT: How do your literature circles work?

VON WEISE: While the other children read silently or wo activities in their journals, I meet with individual lite Within the circle, children share the amazing variety ‹› work they have done in their journals, then we take turns reading the story aloud, about a chapter a day.

A child who is not a fluid reader gets a real sense of the story when the children take turns reading aloud. The good readers listen patiently; everyone is encouraged to read with expression. I believe strongly in developing skills of effective oral interpretation of literature. Reading aloud in literature circles is one way to do this.

RUBRIGHT: Have Dana's reading skills improved?

VON WEISE: Dana still goes to her special reading teacher. She brought a book she has been working on to read to our class. She read it well. I was amazed! The class has discovered her sense of humor, and has become an appreciative audience. Dana has found her niche.

RUBRIGHT: Have other children shown improvement from the improvisational storytelling?

VON WEISE: Several children have grown tremendously. Storytelling has helped them use their own experiences to make learning meaningful. They say, "I'm important. Look! My experiences are valuable. My ideas are good. I have a story; I am going to tell it." This is another reason the family folklore unit is valuable. It is a way for children to get in touch with their life experiences and be able to express them orally and through writing.

It would be interesting to research how children improve their basic reading-writing skills through storytelling and improvised dramatic play.

USING MULTICULTURAL LITERATURE

RUBRIGHT: How do you choose literature that you read or present to your students in their literature circles?

VON WEISE: It has always been important to me to use culturally diverse literature in the classroom. I try to present books in which there are male and female heroes. Some books, like *My Side of the Mountain* [George], have main characters that inspire both my boys and girls.

Other books have female characters that must break through very strong social barriers that say "women can't do this." In Scott O'Dell's

The Island of the Blue Dolphins, Karana, the main character, must overcome tribal traditions in order to make a life for herself. She grows. This growth is reflected in her learning to trust herself and others as she struggles to reach her goals. This is a powerful message for children. They identify with the literary characters struggling with these issues.

RUBRIGHT: There seems to be an emphasis today on literature that confronts subjects like illness and death. Is it important that children face these issues at a young age?

VON WEISE: Good children's literature deals with the spectrum of human experience, including death and illness. In Pearl Buck's *The Big Wave,* the Japanese people face terrible catastrophes like tsunami waves, earthquakes, and erupting volcanoes. Kino's father teaches his son that human perseverance, in spite of fear, is essential for one to live a harmonious life in spite of constant danger from cataclysmic natural disasters.

I like books that show a character's growth and development by solving serious problems. So many characters in quality literature model a range of behaviors for readers. My hope is that when children face serious problems in their own lives, they will remember how certain literary characters responded to similar challenges.

RUBRIGHT: Adults from various ethnic backgrounds tell me that when they were growing up, they rarely encountered role models in literature taught in schools that help them understand and appreciate their cultural identities.

VON WEISE: This is the reason why it is so important to use literature with children from many cultural perspectives, rather than relying on watered-down material often found in basal readers.

Since I have children from many cultures in my classes, it is vital that they have opportunities to see various cultures reflected in the material we read. But they also need to learn how to empathize with people struggling with issues within a culture far different from their own. Literature can help children recognize our vast similarities as humans, while learning to respect and develop tolerance for our cultural differences.

RUBRIGHT: What about children who are not committed to reading? How can you be sure they understand the meaning of stories to the depth that you would like?

VON WEISE: We role-play, storytell, and create informal plays to act out certain scenes. Such dramatic play helps children see how the characters experience a growth process that shapes a fuller, wiser person.

It is often through the simple playing of dramatic scenes that children learn how characters make choices about decisions that impact their lives. Children need inspiration. They need to see how characters, as the story unfolds, learn to trust themselves and others, and successfully rise above adversity.

RUBRIGHT: What about dialect?

VON WEISE: When children hear dialects in the books we read, they discover the tremendous varieties of expression, often lilting, often musical, often poetic, within the English language. *The Secret Garden* [Burnett] and *Flossie and the Fox* [McKissack] come to mind. Often children hear dialects at home that differ from standard English taught at school. They need to know that both forms of expression are valid, important, and mirror cultural differences. Books in which characters speak in dialect demonstrate this to children.

POETRY

RUBRIGHT: Do children read poetry in the literature circles?

VON WEISE: We study poetry together as a class. Poetry shows children the value and beauty of carefully chosen words. Poetry vividly demonstrates the power of putting words together in surprising ways to create mental pictures. It helps the reader see things differently.

Children bring meaning to poems drawn from their own experiences. It is a joy to watch children discover different meanings in a poem, depending on their frame of reference and their insights. Of course, poetry is wonderful for helping children peek into different cultures. I have found that after we read poetry and study how the poet has used so few words to create wonderful mental images, the children want to write their own.

Whether children are writing poetry or prose, I help them see that the writing process involves them in the author cycle.

THE AUTHOR CYCLE

RUBRIGHT: What do you mean by the *author cycle?*

VON WEISE: For me, it flows from brainstorming topics on which to write through drafting, editing, and revision stages to the completed work.

RUBRIGHT: Could you describe how you guide the children through the author cycle?

VON WEISE: First, we brainstorm several ideas, then create a *web* that includes the topic, plus many strands, tangents, associated ideas, and directions a theme might take. The children can focus their writing on any aspect of the topic.

Next, they free-write without concern for punctuation, grammar, or spelling. I want to sense their initial excitement and enthusiasm as they find a place to begin to develop their ideas.

Then, I move quickly through the classroom, listening to their first drafts, making suggestions, and asking questions. After the first writing session, each person shares in front of the class.

Then they choose partners, make suggestions, and probe what they don't understand in each other's work.

Next, the children rewrite. I ask questions to help children restructure their work, fine-tuning their composition to make the heart of the story stand out.

When the children read their polished pieces to their peers, they see the importance of an audience. When an audience accepts a child's writing as meaningful, the writing cycle is complete.

RUBRIGHT: What happens when the writing project is finished?

VON WEISE: After the children illustrate and publish their pieces in book form, we have a celebration for authors where the children act out their stories or read them to one another.

RUBRIGHT: I have heard you say, "I expect the moon and they give it to me." What do you mean?

VON WEISE: I give my very best to the children. I expect them to give me their best, too. Not for *me,* but for *themselves.* They seem to understand that my high expectations for quality work are to help them become good writers.

RUBRIGHT: You have a gift of motivating your children. What is your secret?

VON WEISE: Humor and enthusiasm. We have fun. I believe that you have to be eager to learn. You have to want it. And if my children don't have this hunger for learning, I try to create it. Learning is what life is about. I want my students to develop a lifetime passion for learning. The arts are often the magic door to this world of the imagination and knowledge.

14

Artist-in-Residence Programs

METRO THEATER CIRCUS (MTC)

When creative drama specialist Zaro Weil came to my classroom in 1971 to explore new modes to "teach" drama, mime, movement, puppetry, and music, my upper elementary students were delighted. I didn't realize that what we were modeling with our Thursday afternoon sessions were some of the country's first artist-in-residence programs. Previously, I had not heard the word *residency*, and knew nothing of the Missouri Arts Council's interest in funding artists to work in schools.

After months of play with my students, exploring how the arts could be more integral to my lesson plans, Zaro suggested that I quit my teaching job at the end of the year to cofound a touring children's theater company, Metro Theater Circus (MTC). (It flourishes today as Metro Theater Company.)

Zaro located free studio space in a large empty private school classroom in St. Louis in exchange for our teaching theater arts. Since I was neither a mime nor a dancer, Zaro suggested I "teach" storytelling. From long-playing records, I learned stories, entered the classrooms, and told them. For me, this was an awakening about storytelling's great potential. Before long, the children and I were making up stories from ideas they posed. Thus began the improvisational story-building exercise that I call story weaving. Soon story weaving was a regular part of MTC performances.

To enhance the educational side of MTC's offering, we mailed advance materials to schools to prepare both teachers and students for what they were to see at a MTC performance, listing suggestions for follow-up classroom activities. (MTC received the Winifred Ward Prize for the best new children's theater in America in 1973.)

UNIVERSITY OF WINCHESTER
LIBRARY

Residencies

Our troupe discovered that Missouri Arts Council funding not only helped schools finance our performances, but made it possible for us to offer residency programs. We learned that all states maintain arts councils to support residencies, although guidelines differ somewhat. In schools without art or music specialists, residencies may be a student's only formal involvement with the arts or artists.

Generally, state residency guidelines stipulate that studio space be provided to sculptors, dancers, potters, painters, and other artists so students can observe the artist at work. During a residency, each artist must teach small groups of children the fundamentals of his or her art form. Residencies can span a few hours in one day, a week, a month, or the entire school year—there is no prescribed time limit. But committing large blocks of time is often impossible for a busy artist. Some schools decide that it is better to bypass the arts agency and book an artist directly.

Ann Moe, an art teacher at McKinley Elementary School in Appleton, Wisconsin, recalls that in a two-day residency, her school PTO funded sculptor Dallas Anderson. He began the residency by spending several hours on the school playground observing until he found the perfect child to use as a model to sculpt in clay.

At an all-school lecture-demonstration, Anderson crafted a twenty-inch wire armature of his model, a fifth-grade boy wearing a baseball cap holding a basketball in one hand, a Coke in the other. Anderson sculpted on a revolving modeling stand so the children, seated on the gym floor, could gain unrestricted views of his wire shaping.

Later on, each class visited Anderson's makeshift studio to watch him apply oil-base clay to the wire armature.

"Who got the statue?" I asked. "The sculptor," Moe replied. "It was displayed for a month in a hall showcase. The sculptor offered to cast the clay form in bronze for the parents, but the cost was prohibitive."

Moe had prepared her art classes for the sculptor's visit by sharing illustrations of sculptures. Following the residency, her classes made their own sculptures from oil-base clay.

Every residency differs. All require the imagination and commitment of an administrator, faculty member, or parent volunteer to initiate planning and determine whom to invite as well as how to plot and finance the program. All program outlines need to list expected learning outcomes and benefits to students and teachers.

After several years with MTC, I left to become a professional story-teller and fine arts consultant with a specialty of assisting schools and districts in establishing arts residencies.

Many artists are not able to commit time to an extensive residency, but are willing to work with specific teachers to enrich and expand the curriculum. For example, St. Louis poet Constance Levy often visits classrooms to lead poetry writing sessions. Planning with Levy, the teachers and their students study poems prior to Levy's formal visit. During consecutive weekly sessions, Levy reads her own and others' poetry and supervises classroom poetry writing workshops that are often funded by the PTO.

Between live appearances by artists during residencies, teachers can keep residencies alive with films and videos, field trips, storytelling from related texts, and other tailored projects that fit the residency topic.

TWO RESIDENCY PROGRAMS

Making Steel Drums: A High School Residency

When I spotted Oswald Moses, a Trinidadian singer, storyteller, folk musician, and steel drum player on the arts council performance roster, I invited him to brainstorm how he might work with high school students. Moses said he'd prefer a group of students working alongside him to build a set of steel drums such as are popular in Trinidad today.

Our high school principal was skeptical about the idea, but the band director saw its merits. We were given a green light to move ahead. Moses and his twelve-student crew received permission to build their drums on the banks of a river that ran through a city park.

Shell Oil donated and delivered six new steel oil drums to the park site. Moses and his crew sawed the drums in halves and thirds, creating the basic shape for the pans. Then, they tempered the pans over an open fire, banging them with sledge hammers until the heads became malleable, and notes could be played on them with mallets.

While fashioning the steel drums, Moses shared songs and stories from Trinidad. After World War II, he explained, steel drums containing oil for American bases in the Caribbean were left behind as surplus. Ingenious islanders figured out how to use them as musical drums.

Moses taught his team of high school students how to play the drums. For a residency finale, the Moses group presented a steel drum band concert on the stage of the St. Louis Art Museum.

Beyond booking artists like Moses for special residencies in school districts, I sometimes served as guest storyteller-in-residence for other schools and districts.

An All-School Storytelling Residency

Prior to a one-week, all-school storytelling residency in Appleton, Wisconsin, the arts committee asked me to be sure to involve the gym teacher, counselors, speech therapists, Title I resource teachers, art and music specialists, and librarian, in addition to classroom teachers.

By phone and mail we designed curriculum that bridged language arts and social studies and included art, movement, music, geography, history, science, and math for each grade level. Study topics chosen by each grade were:

Kindergarten and grade one: "Ananse the Spider," tales to help learn about the Ashanti people of Ghana, West Africa.
Prekindergarten and second grade: Arnold Lobel's *Frog and Toad;* stories to develop a science and creative writing unit on frogs and toads.
Grades three and four: Lore, legend, tall tales, to study Wisconsin history from the 1800s.
Grades five and six: Norse mythology as a springboard to study history, lore, and legend of Iceland.

When I arrived for a preresidency all-day in-service teacher training workshop, teachers reported that their classes were immersed in the prechosen residency topics. In the workshop, teachers learned short folktales using the quick-and-easy method so they could tell tales in their classrooms when the residency formally opened. They also taught their own students to learn tales the same way (see Chapter Eight).

On the first day of the residency, the school secretary rushed me up to the library. "You've got to see this," she exclaimed. "The principal is telling a story to the fifth and sixth graders!" That same day, several teachers reported early success in their very first classroom storytelling efforts.

The basic artist-in-residence format throughout the week was for me to give two or three large performances daily to a grade or two at a time, then following each performance to systematically visit individual classrooms for questions, personal coaching in storytelling, exercises, and observation.

Extending the Stories

During the week, prekindergartners and second graders wrote and illustrated story sequels to Lobel's *Frog and Toad* stories. They offered me their homemade toad cookies as they took turns reading aloud their sequels.

Sandra Miller and her third- and fourth-grade team teachers focused on Wisconsin folklore, especially nineteenth-century ghost tales.

I told Miller's classes a tall tale, with sound effects, about an Ozark monster who lived in a cave that he had gouged out by hand hundreds of years ago. "How do you make those strange noises?" asked one student. "Some sounds come naturally to me," I answered, "but I always practice special noises to make the story I'm telling more interesting."

Later, I found Miller leading a "sound-making workshop" so her class could bring their own stories to life. Miller's students invited me to their class storytelling festival toward week's end. "Come early, we're having a Paul Bunyan breakfast with pancakes and sausage."

In a plaid shirt, red suspenders, jeans and boots, Miller greeted me at the door with a cup of coffee and a plate of sausages and pancakes. "Come on in. The storytelling is about to begin," she said. Class members wore blue jeans, plaid shirts, neck scarves, and suspenders.

Later that day, I observed Miller's students enacting folk dances of early Wisconsin settlement days that they had learned in gym class, where the gym teacher introduced them to new story games he had devised.

One day Jane Anderson-Wood, a specialist in learning disabilities, stopped me in the hall. She feared that some of her poorer reading students would not be able to read the short folktales I had recommended for the storytelling workshop she planned to conduct with them.

Although I gave her copies of a story the children had heard in assembly, she remained apprehensive. Nonetheless, she proceeded with the workshop. Later, she hailed me again. "Not only could they read that story, they added their own sounds. I watched their self-confidence growing before my eyes."

I was not surprised. Teachers who work with poor readers are often stunned to discover how well students read once they have heard stories told.

The fifth and sixth graders were involved in video studies of Icelandic history and lore by the time I arrived. I personalized content on the videos by telling stories about my own visits to Iceland. I recounted a walk on a mountain of volcanic ash, a contemporary Icelandic fisherman story, and Norse myths that were recorded in Iceland in the 1200s.

A fifth-grade boy requested that I tell more stories about "Thor the Thunder god." I told him that there just wasn't time to schedule another storytelling session. "That's okay," he said, "I found one in the library and read it myself." I suggested that he learn the story to tell to the class himself. As we walked down the hall he said, "You know, I didn't even *like* Iceland before you came and started to tell us stories from there. Now I *love* it!"

At McKinley School, the residency's success depended on the entire staff, the principal's support, and months of planning—but mainly on the vision and commitment of both residency coordinators, Anderson-Wood and Miller.

Although many artist-in-schools programs are made possible through financial support from local, state, or regional arts councils, the McKinley storytelling residency was funded almost entirely by its PTO, with additional help from the principal's fund, and the district's discretionary monies for developing improvement in reading instruction.

(See Bibliography for addresses of agencies and organizations providing information about artist-in-residence programs.)

15

Stories to Tell—Quick and Easy

JACK AND THE BEANSTALK

Adapted by Lynn Rubright

Jack and his mother lived in a small cottage in the rolling English countryside. They had a few chickens, a small garden, and a cow, Milky White, who had stopped giving milk.

So it wasn't surprising when one day, Jack's mother said, "Jack, there is nothing in the house to eat. You'll have to take Milky White to market and sell her for the best price you can get."

"Ah, Mum," said Jack, "maybe I could get a job, instead of selling the cow." After all, Jack and Milky White, who had grown up together, had grown quite fond of one another. "Jack, don't argue. Besides, you've tried to get a job before and no one would have you. There are no jobs to be had." So, promising his mother that he would get a good price, Jack set off to market to sell Milky White.

He hadn't gone far when, from nowhere it seemed, a little man appeared in his path. "How do ye do, Jack?"

"How do you know my name?" asked Jack, startled.

"There's lots that I know about you, son. You're on your way to sell the cow at market, are you not?" Jack nodded. But he was even more surprised when the little man said, "And your mum made you promise to get a good price for her, too. Well, perhaps I can be of help. Here in my hand I have five beans." The little man held out his hand. Jack saw that each one was a different size and a different color.

"These are magic beans, Jack. And if you trade me Milky White for the magic beans, I guarantee that your luck will change."

Jack had been hoping his luck would change for a long while, and when the little man told him the beans would bring good luck, he thought that was a good price for a cow that didn't give milk. Jack traded Milky White for the five magic beans and hurried home to tell his mother of their good fortune.

"Magic beans?" yelled his mother. "You good-for-nothing, foolish boy. I'll show you what you do with magic beans." With that, his mother opened the kitchen window and flung the beans into the garden. "Not enough to fix for dinner. Not enough for a mouthful. Up to bed, you silly boy, and without a bite of supper."

Poor Jack wept a tear or two, for his stomach was empty, but soon he fell asleep. And strange dreams he had, too, but not as strange as what he saw when he woke up. Something green—greener than the grass in the meadow—was growing right outside his window. Jack jumped up and opened the window. It was a bean tree! Its tangled vines seemed to sing, "Come, climb up upon my leafy stalk. When you get to the top you can take a walk."

Jack may have been a lazy boy, but he tried to be obedient. Without so much as a thought for his mother, Jack was out the window and climbing up and up and up the tall green stem. Soon he was in the clouds where the stalk was thin, swaying to and fro. "Jump, Jack, jump!" it commanded. Jack was the type of fellow who often leaped before he looked, and he did so now, without so much as a thought. Which shouldn't surprise you.

Jack was amazed to find himself on a road, right in the midst of the clouds. His mother was always saying, "Just follow your nose, son, and you won't get lost." Jack was already lost, but he thought it best to follow his nose anyway. His nose led him right to a mansion. There it stood, shiny gold turrets poking into the blue of the sky. He hoisted himself up the steep steps and, on tiptoes, banged the brass knocker. The door squeaked open, and there loomed the largest woman in the world. "Well!" she bellowed. "What do you want?"

"Please Mum, I've come so far. Have you a crust of bread and a drop of milk? I haven't eaten for over a day." She bid him in and nudged him toward her husband's mountainous chair. Not an easy climb, but since he had just scaled a beanstalk, he managed fine. Resting on the cushion seat, Jack nibbled on a crust of bread as large as his mother's loaf, and drank milk from the good woman's thimble. "More milk than Milky White had given in a month," Jack thought. "My luck has begun to change already."

But just then a roar shook the great house. "Fee Fi Fo Fum, I smell the blood of an Englishman. Be he alive or be he dead, I'll grind his bones to make my bread."

"I think that means me," said Jack, scurrying down from the chair and popping himself into the oven, just as the giant entered the room. "Nonsense, my dear. You just smell the boy you broiled on toast yesterday," said the good wife. With that she brought him roast beef, potatoes and gravy, pudding, and ale. After he had filled his belly, the giant spread out his gold coins, which he counted and measured before putting them back in the sack, barely tying it up before falling asleep. The poor giant's wife, who had forgotten all about Jack, was out back scrubbing dishes.

"A bit more luck," thought Jack, who sneaked out of the oven, climbed up the carved table leg, and grabbed the heavy sack of gold before slipping through the crack in the great door. Bouncing down the steps, he raced toward the slip of green he saw peeking though the clouds. The beanstalk seemed to shout, "Hurry Jack, hurry back, with the sack of gold." Sliding down the stalk, he landed with a bump. And there stood his mother with a scowl on her face. "Jack! Where have you been?"

When Jack showed her the sack of gold, her voice softened. "Perhaps you are a chip off the old block, after all." Jack didn't know whether or not he was a chip off a block, but he liked her tone of voice, so he didn't say anything. He even promised never to go up the beanstalk again.

That is, until one morning he was awakened by the beckoning call of the beanstalk. "Come on Jack, time to climb again." Before he could tell his mother, the beanstalk drew him into its leaves and nudged him upward, upward toward the clouds. Now that he knew the way, he didn't have to follow his nose. He made his way straight to the mansion. But the wife wasn't about to let another fellow inside who might steal something like the last boy who had visited.

"Please, Mum, I've come so far." She had a soft heart. Besides, what good had the giant's money ever done her? All he ever did with it was count it after supper, and put it back in the sack. Jack had no sooner taken a bite of cold pudding when the giant returned, yelling, "Fee Fi Fo Fum." None too soon, Jack jumped into a cooking pot, leaving the lid open a crack from which to peek. When his wife brought in a steaming platter of food, the giant forgot about little boys broiled on toast.

After a hearty supper, the giant fetched his hen. Jack was amazed when the giant said, "Lay, hen, lay!" and a perfectly beautiful golden egg appeared on the table, which the giant stashed in his pocket. "Lovely," said Jack, "I must have her." Jack knew all about hens, as he had raised a few himself. When the giant fell asleep, Jack sneaked from his hiding place, grabbed the hen, and tucked her head under his arm before she could squawk. Once more he ran to the beanstalk, which said, "Hurry with the hen, my boy. The giant's pet will soon be missed."

Jack slid down the stalk in a flash, but his angry mother said, "Jack, you promised never to climb that bean plant again." Jack said, "Lay, hen, lay." With a cluck, cluck, cluck and a squawk, squawk, squawk, a golden egg was laid. "Jack! You are indeed a chip off the old block." If it means to get lucky, Jack thought he might be a chip off the block. Soon there were new curtains at the windows, food in the cupboard, and a fancy hen on a velvet cushion at the foot of Jack's bed.

Then one day the beanstalk called again. "One more time, Jack; just one more climb." In no time Jack was back at the castle gate. This time he didn't knock. The door was open a crack, and in he slid. Right under the sink he hid. Nobody even noticed the smell of boy, for the wife had made a dinner so fine the aroma filled the room. Turkey roast and sage dressing, sweet potato soufflé, mustard greens, and pumpkin pie.

"Oh my," said Jack, his mouth watering and stomach growling. But hunger was forgotten when the giant asked his golden harp for a lullaby.

Jack was in love. He had to have her. But this time when he took the giant's treasure, the harp called, "Master, master, help me!" The giant woke up and ran after his golden treasure. "Ah," sighed his wife, "he never runs after me like that. Wouldn't, even if I were stolen." With lumbering strides, the giant was overtaking Jack. "Jump, boy, quick, slide down the stalk." Jack hollered, "Mother, Mother, bring the ax!" For once, Jack gave the order, and his mother obeyed. Indeed, his luck had changed.

Jack handed the harp to his mother in exchange for the ax. As the great feet came closer and closer to the ground, Jack chopped, faster and faster—until the great stalk came crashing. The giant smashed to earth. The giant's wife, who had followed the chase, peered at the spectacle through the hole in the clouds. "Humm!" she thought. "There he lies embedded in earth, entwined in greens. He looks quite dead." He was. But what became of the dead giant's body and his good wife are tales for another day.

I can tell you this. Jack and his mother did live happily for a long while; in time, the harp was happy, too. The little man was right; the beans had changed Jack's luck. Jack was convinced that he was a chip off the old block, after all. But of course that isn't the end of tales about Jack.

BELLEROPHON AND PEGASUS: A GREEK MYTH

Bellerophon was a great trainer of horses. Hoping to catch and tame the wonderful winged horse, Pegasus, for his own, Bellerophon practiced roping wild stallions with his lasso.

But Pegasus was swift and no one, not even Bellerophon, could catch him.

One night Bellerophon went to the temple of Athena to ask for help, but he fell asleep. He dreamed he caught Pegasus by throwing a golden bridle and reins over his head. In his dream he rode Pegasus over the islands of Greece. When he woke up a golden bridle lay in his hands—a gift from Athena herself!

For many days Bellerophon searched the sky for a sign of Pegasus. But he never saw the flying horse.

Then one day when Bellerophon was in Corinth he saw the glorious animal drinking from a nearby stream.

Very quietly, Bellerophon crept up behind him. But Pegasus, seeing Bellerophon's reflection in the water, arched his great wings for flight. Too late! Bellerophon flung the golden bridle over his neck. Immediately, it began to work its magic.

Amazingly, the winged horse tucked his wings against his side and stood still. Pegasus and Bellerophon looked at each other. Bellerophon petted his soft nose and spoke quietly to the marvelous horse.

Holding the golden reins, Bellerophon jumped onto his back. "Fly!" he commanded Pegasus, nudging his heels and knees into the horse's flanks.

Arching his glorious wings, Pegasus obeyed. Together they spiraled higher and higher. Soaring up, swooping down, around and around they flew.

Bellerophon and Pegasus became inseparable. They had many adventures together. But none so famous as the time Bellerophon freed the people of Lycia from the torment of the terrible monster called Chimera—a fire-breathing creature with the head of a lion, body of a goat, and tail of a serpent. Pegasus swept down toward the fire-breathing monster as Bellerophon, clutching his mane, plunged a spear tipped with molten iron down the creature's throat and killed him.

Bellerophon married the beautiful daughter of the grateful king of Lycia and in time became himself a beloved king and ruler of the kingdom.

Unfortunately, Bellerophon became so proud of his power and the spectacular deeds he did with Pegasus that he began to think he was as powerful as the gods. One day, Bellerophon urged Pegasus to fly him to Mount Olympus. Higher and higher he coaxed Pegasus to fly—but an enraged Zeus sent a fly to bite Pegasus. The horse bolted from the sting, pitching Bellerophon through the air. Falling to earth, Bellerophon landed in a bed of briars in a land far from his home.

Pegasus stayed on Mount Olympus and served Zeus by delivering his thunder and lightning bolts to him. But the poor, lame Bellerophon wandered as a humble beggar the rest of his days.

AESOP'S FABLES—RETOLD BY LYNN RUBRIGHT

The Goose That Laid Golden Eggs

Once there was a farmer who had a goose who faithfully laid an egg every day. One day she astonished the farmer by laying an egg that was solid gold.

"Amazing," thought the farmer, who ran to show the treasure to his wife. Now this farmer was not a rich man, and the golden egg was a great gift. He said to his wife, "Now we will be able to make repairs to the house and barn." His wife was delighted, too. "And I shall make curtains and buy new furniture."

The next day the goose laid another golden egg. "Look! More gold," said the farmer to his wife. "Perhaps we should sell this old place and get a new one."

"You are right," she replied. "Why should I put new furniture in this old house?" But before they had a chance to do anything, the goose laid another golden egg. The farmer and his wife discussed their riches. "Now I will be able to buy more land, raise more crops."

The farmer began to wonder how many golden eggs the goose might lay. He said to his wife, "If my goose lays a golden egg every day, think about how many golden eggs she must have inside herself. Why not kill her now and get them all at once? Then we will be truly rich."

His wife, who now had more than she ever thought she would have in this life, was not as foolish as her husband. She said, "But we have plenty now. Why not be content with what we have, and be grateful for whatever more that comes?"

But her husband could not let the idea go. He dreamed of great wealth and believed that he could have it all at once if only he killed the goose. The next day he took his ax, went into the barn, and killed the goose. When he cut her open he was horrified to see that she had no golden eggs inside her at all.

In his hurry to kill the goose he hadn't bothered to see whether or not she had laid another golden egg that morning. Under her dead body there it was—the last golden egg. The farmer saw how his greed had killed the goose that laid golden eggs. His wife shook her head. She prepared the dead goose for dinner, stuffing and baking her into a pie. Her husband ate it sadly, confessing how foolish he had been. From that time forth every time they had goose for dinner, they called it "humble pie."

The Meeting of the Mice

"There must be a way to keep the cat from chasing us," said the mayor mouse. "Our lives are made miserable by his stalking us. Does anyone have an idea what we might do?"

No one said a word, as this was a very old problem that was often discussed during mouse meetings. "Since cat paws are so quiet, we don't have a chance," said a young mouse. "Why not think of a way to make him noisy?"

All the mice laughed, but the mayor said, "She may have a point. What do you have in mind, young lady?"

"All we need to do is put a bell around the cat's neck," she continued. "Then we'll know exactly where he is at all times."

Everyone agreed that it was a wonderful idea. If they could bell the cat, the mice would always hear when it was near. After a discussion, the proposition to bell the cat won by a unanimous vote. Great Grandfather Mouse did not vote as he seemed to be sleeping, something he often did at meetings. Everyone congratulated the young mouse on her insight and applauded her wisdom.

After it was agreed that the cat must wear a bell to warn them of danger approaching, it was decided to form a committee to do the deed. The mayor asked, "And who will serve on the committee to bell the cat?" Not a mouse paw was raised.

"If there are no volunteers, I will have to appoint a committee to carry out the task. Miss Mouse, since it was your idea, I appoint you chair of the Cat Belling Committee."

"O sir," interceded the little mouse's mother, "she is far too young, and has never served on a committee. It takes a great deal of experience to chair a committee."

"Well, then how about you, Madam Mouse?" said the mayor. "Oh, sir, there is too much risk. Little Mouse is my only daughter. If something happens to me how will she survive?" With that, everyone realized the danger involved. All mouse eyes turned away, as the mayor pleaded for volunteers. Only then did Great Grandfather Mouse speak. He hadn't been sleeping at all.

"I have lived with this cat problem all my life," he said. "It's been discussed for generations. Although you have a good idea, Miss Mouse, you have discovered something that I learned long ago. It is easier to say you will do something than to do it."

The meeting was adjourned, but not before several mice agreed to serve on a committee to further study the resolution to bell the cat.

The Milkmaid's Dream

"Molly, time to milk the cow!" called her mother. But filling the bucket with frothy cow's milk was only part of Molly's chore. Taking the milk to market to sell was another of her duties.

Since she and her mother were poor, Molly's feet were bare, and her dress was patched. Nevertheless, she made a pretty sight walking down the country road. Her golden braids dangled down her back as she balanced the milk pail on her head.

Molly was a dreamer. One day on the way to market, she imagined herself selling the milk for enough money to buy some chicks. Molly saw herself hand-feeding them, and when they were big and plump they would lay many eggs. Then she could sell the eggs and get enough money to make a dress with store-bought cloth. And there would be extra money for a petticoat, and parasol of lace, and shoes of imported leather.

"I will look so fine, I will be asked to the dance. And at the dance the fiddler will play, and I will swirl and twirl like this." Molly did a spin in the road, lost her balance, and the milk pail came tumbling down, spilling the sweet milk on the ground.

"All is lost," she cried, running back home in tears. Molly told her story to her mother, who loved her despite her foolishness. "Molly, my girl, it's a waste of time to cry over spilt milk. What good does that do? It also does no good to count chickens before they're hatched, now does it? Stop crying, girl, tomorrow's another day when the cow must be milked again. Who knows, maybe your dreams will come true by and by."

The Stork and the Fox

Fox had always admired Stork, who was tall, stately, dignified. Fox was not jealous of the stork, just intrigued by her manner. Each step she took was so calculated as she bent her knees, placing her feet primly as she strutted. Fox invited Stork to dinner to get better acquainted. Since Fox loved his food almost as much as he loved himself, he wanted to be sure that she wouldn't eat too much.

Knowing that Stork had a very long bill, he served a delicious soup in a shallow bowl. "There," thought Fox, "now I can enjoy Stork's company, and be sure she won't eat everything up too quickly."

When Stork arrived, Fox saw how proper she was. But when they sat for dinner, Fox found her less than a good conversationalist. She was far too busy concentrating on how she might sip even a little of the fine soup Fox had served in such a shallow soup bowl. The tip of her bill barely got wet, and stork got very little to eat that night.

Hiding her irritation, the stork invited the fox to dinner the very next evening. How pleased he was. "She likes me, or why would she have invited me to dinner so soon?" Fox brushed his coat and fluffed his tail. He polished his teeth until they gleamed. After preening, he proudly loped off to the dinner party.

Greeting him, Stork bowed her graceful neck. Fox smelled the glorious stew. His mouth watered; he drooled in an ungentlemanly manner. Stork delayed serving dinner, preferring to visit. But Fox was in no mood for small talk.

Finally, Stork invited Fox to the table, where she served the stew in tall glasses. Stork had no trouble sticking her long beak into the glass for tasty morsels of spicy meat. Charmingly, she chattered about the weather as she savored her delicious meal. When Fox tried to get his snout into the glass he discovered that his nose was too wide. He looked so comical trying to eat stew from a glass, Stork could barely hold back her laughter. But she only smiled as she continued to eat and chat.

Finally Fox, weak from hunger and overcome with frustration, excused himself. "You will have to forgive me, Stork, but I have a pressing appointment."

"Fox, you have not finished your stew, did you not like it?" she called out to him. If Fox answered, she had no idea what he said, for Stork was by now laughing so hard she wouldn't have been able to hear a word.

Dog and Wolf

Once a scrawny wolf was loping past a farmhouse when he noticed a well-fed dog sleeping in a fenced-in yard. "Hello! " called the wolf to the dog, waking him up. "Fine day for a nap."

Dog woke up, stretched, then trotted over to the fence where Wolf stood. "Why, yes," Dog said, "it is nice to catch a few winks now and again."

By now Wolf was feeling not a little jealous. "And that little house there in the yard, I suppose you can go in there when it rains or snows."

"Indeed, it is my very own house," replied Dog, sensing envy in Wolf's voice and feeling quite fortunate.

"And those big bowls by your little house. I suppose they are for food?" asked Wolf, his mouth watering.

"Yes," said Dog. "One is for water and one is for food. They are filled to the brim once a day. I have never gone hungry in my life." Then Dog looked closely at Wolf. His coat was scraggly and worn, and he was so thin his ribs showed through the fur.

"And what must you do to deserve such care and comfort?" asked Wolf. "Surely such riches do not come without a price."

"Well," admitted the dog, "I do have a few duties. I must watch the house when Mistress is away. I must tend the sheep when they are in the meadow, to keep them safe from fellows like you. And I must chase away anyone who comes near the house uninvited."

"Hum," said the Wolf, "sounds like a lot of work for your pay. And what is wrong with your neck? There is little fur growing there."

"Well," said the dog, embarrassed, "sometimes Master chains me up so I will not run away—not that I have ever thought of such a thing. And Mistress puts me on a leash when we go marketing. Wolf saw a metal chain attached to a leather collar lying on the ground.

Wolf threw back his head and laughed. "So being fenced in, tied up, and obedient to your masters is the price you pay for food and shelter." Dog nodded. He had never thought of his life in that light before. "For myself," said Wolf, "I'd rather be free to roam when and where I wish. Although I suffer now and again from an empty stomach, it is a small price for freedom." With that Wolf was off with a bound into the woods.

Dog, hearing his master's whistle, ran off to serve him without thinking much about what the wolf had said. He was much too busy.

The Frog and the Ox

Mr. Frog was elegant indeed, attired in his finest waistcoat, silk neck scarf, spats, and high-top leather boots. He carried a walking stick which he thrust proudly before him as he strolled. Frog was so busy tipping his hat to creatures who crossed his path he barely saw a small toad who said, "Good morning, Mr. Frog, have you seen the fine ox grazing in the meadow? He must be new to the neighborhood. I have never seen anything so large and fine as that ox."

"Really, Toad, just how big and fine is this ox you have observed? This big?" Frog threw back his head and filled the air sack under his chin until it ballooned.

"Oh much bigger than that, Mr. Frog. This ox is so tall he blocks out the sun. And he is so wide that a hundred frogs could sit upon his back."

"Perhaps Ox is more like this, then." Frog puffed himself up even larger, stretching on his tiptoes to seem taller.

"Oh, bigger, Mr. Frog," said Toad. "Ox is *much* bigger than that."

"Like this?" Mr. Frog filled his air pouch so *big* and stretched himself so tall that he *exploded!* And all that was left of Mr. Frog was a leather boot here and there, and his silk scarf dangling from the bush. "No, even bigger than that," said the little toad, who wondered where Mr. Frog had gone.

The Oak and the Reed

Once a fine oak tree lived by the side of a small stream. He had lived there for over a hundred years, and had a massive trunk and great branches that arched majestically over the water. How proud he was of his strength. He felt indestructible. The oak had survived all kinds of weather for generations. He delighted in teasing the little reed that grew in the marsh near the water's edge. "Look at you, little one," he would chastise her. "Every breeze blows you this way and that. Where is your strength of character?"

"But I like blowing in the breeze," replied the reed. "Look what I can do." With every gust of wind, the reed swayed forward and backward, round and round.

But the oak said, "Just goes to show you don't have backbone like me. Nothing sways me. 'Strong as an oak,' that's what folks say about trees like me. 'Stand tall, stand strong,' that's my motto," bellowed the oak. There wasn't much the supple little reed could say to this. Besides, the oak made her feel a little guilty as she danced in the breeze.

Then one night there came a storm more terrible than anyone had seen in a hundred years. Lighting flashed, rain poured for hours, but worst was the terrible wind. The little reed was buffeted this way and that, bending almost to the earth many, many times. Suddenly, in the middle of the night there was a terrible cracking sound and a deep groaning. The reed was frightened, but it wasn't until morning when the storm had passed and the sun began to creep over the horizon that she saw the great oak tree no longer stood by her side. Instead, on the ground were branches, twigs, and chunks of wood that had been its mighty trunk. The great oak tree had been felled by the storm.

A woodcutter came by with his ax and saw his good fortune.

The little reed watched with sadness as the oak tree was chopped into firewood. She swayed gracefully as the breeze blew her about. "Maybe it's better to be flexible, and blow with the wind. Hum," she thought, "perhaps I have a motto, too."

Fox and the Turkeys

One day a fox was strolling in the wood, wishing that he had a nice juicy dinner to get rid of the growing rumble in his stomach. Then he heard a chorus of gobbling sounds. He looked up and saw five plump turkeys sitting in the tree overhead. His mouth watered; his belly grumbled. "Hello," called the fox, pleasantly. "I've been traveling and haven't talked with a soul for days. Why not drop down for a little visit?"

"Hello, yourself," cried the oldest one. "Your tricks are well known, Mr. Fox. We can visit from our roost. What do you want to talk about?"

"Let me tell you about my recent trip abroad," replied Mr. Fox. "What about it?" asked old Mrs. Turkey, who had a secret yen to travel.

"I've been studying music and dance," said the fox. "Let me sing you a little song, and show you a few steps. You might try them yourself next time you're on the ground." With that the fox began to hum a melody, and did a little dance. First he did the two-step; then he waltzed in circles. When he glanced up and saw the turkeys swaying to the rhythms, he smiled to himself. Then he did a jig, followed with a bit of rock and roll, finishing with his favorite, the fox trot.

It was too much; the turkeys were so busy keeping the beat that one by one they lost their balance, plopped off the branches, and fell to the ground. Mr. Fox stuffed them into his sack, dancing and singing all the way home. His turkey feast lasted days and days.

Mr. Fox and Mr. Crow

Mr. Fox and Mr. Crow were never great friends, but being somewhat similar in nature they respected one another. Both were known for their cleverness. They enjoyed studying each other's wily ways in hopes of becoming smarter themselves.

One day as Mr. Fox was loping through the forest he smelled something delicious. Looking up he saw Mr. Crow sitting in a branch overhead. His strong beak was partway open and in it he clutched the biggest piece of yellow cheese that Mr. Fox had ever seen. Oh, how Fox wanted that cheese, but he only smiled and said, "Ah, Mr. Crow, what a lovely day."

"Hummmm," agreed Crow, nodding his head, squeezing the cheese tightly in his beak.

"And how beautifully your black feathers glisten in the sunlight," said Fox.

"Hummmmm!" Crow nodded, pleased that Fox appreciated the sheen of his coat.

"And how bright your eyes, and strong your claws," said Fox. "Hummmm." Crow nodded again.

"But the cat must have your tongue." Fox laughed. "Your brothers and sisters soar through the sky laughing and singing, but you must have laryngitis. Or maybe you just hate making conversation. I had thought you were famous not just for your beauty but for your voice as well."

With that Crow opened his beak and said, "My voice is every bit as beautiful as my feathers." But when he did so, the luscious piece of cheese fell to the ground and the fox grabbed it, swallowing it down in one gulp. "My cheese! You stole it! Give it back this instant!" cawed the crow in his most unpleasant cry.

"Oh dear," said the fox, "I thought you said you had a fine voice. That screeching is most unbecoming. Truly a hardship on my ears." And with that the laughing fox ran away with Crow's cheese. The crow darted this way and that searching for the fox as he *caw cawed* the most unpleasant sound in the wood. Crow was furious that he had been tricked by Mr. Fox's flattery.

The Wild Boar and the Fox

Fox seemed interested in everyone and everything. When he wasn't hungry, tricking everybody into sharing a bit of food, he was curiously observing life around him. One day, as he traveled along a hedgerow at the meadow's edge, he came upon a wild boar. Wild boars are ornery, cantankerous beasts, and it is a good idea to give them a wide berth. But this wild boar was busy sharpening his tusks on the trunk of a tree, and the fox was curious.

"Excuse me, sir," said the fox. "You have such magnificent tusks, why do you sharpen them further? Are there huntsmen in these woods?" For a moment the wild boar glared at the fox with his little pig eyes. Fox took a step back, glancing which way he might retreat in a hurry.

"No!" snorted the boar. "No huntsmen today that I have seen."

"Then why waste your time sharpening your tusks?" asked the fox. "The day is a fine one, and I know a watering hole not far from here where you can wallow in the mud, and enjoy the sun. Why not come with me? I'm on my way there now."

"Sorry, young fellow, I have work to do. I have survived thus far by being ready when the hunters come. They are stealthy and quick, and it will be too late to sharpen my tusks when they are upon me. I must be prepared."

The fox thought this might be a very good plan for the wild boar, but not for him, so he hurried off to the watering hole for a swim.

Grasshopper and the Owl

Old Owl loved to sleep, especially during the day. At night he was busy, catching his dinner, but by day he liked to sleep, and he didn't like noisy neighbors. So when Grasshopper began to sing in his raspy voice, owl's sleep was disturbed. "Quiet, please," he called.

"Sorry," answered Grasshopper from his hiding place in the tree's trunk. For a moment all was quiet. Owl had no sooner dozed off when Grasshopper began his song again. If you know anything about grasshoppers, this shouldn't surprise you. By nature they love to sing, and can hardly keep themselves from doing so.

"Quiet, please!" called Owl, irritated at being disturbed once more. "Sorry," replied Grasshopper, who made a serious attempt to be still. But as soon as Owl was asleep, Grasshopper began again.

"Certainly it's useless to call *quiet*," thought the angry owl, as he gave the matter some thought. Sweetly Owl said to the grasshopper, "Friend, since you love to sing so, would you like to accompany me to the meadow? I know of some particularly sweet flowers whose nectar would give you something to sing about. Hop out from your nesting place, and I will give you a ride there on my back."

Grasshopper jumped out of the crevice where had tucked himself and looked up at Owl. "Delighted, sir," he said. With that Owl swept swiftly from his perch popped the grasshopper into his mouth, swallowing him down with one gulp. "Now, for some peace and quiet!" thought Owl, as he settled down for an undisturbed sleep.

Sour Grapes

Fox was loping along when suddenly his stomach told him that it was hungry. "What is this you say, stomach? That you are in need of sustenance?" His nose answered with a sniff. Fox said, "Nose, are you telling me that food is near? His eyes looked up and saw grapes hanging from a vine. Fox felt his mouth water.

"Humm!" said Fox. "Good stomach, fine nose, dear mouth, you tell me good things to eat are near. Sweet, ripe grapes hanging from the vine. Feet, you know what to do. Jump!" And so Fox's feet jumped higher and higher. The closer he came the more his stomach growled; the more saliva dripped from his lips; the more his eyes gleamed with desire.

Fox wanted those grapes. But no mattter how high Fox jumped, he could not get the grapes. Finally, he fell down, exhausted. "Well, what are you looking at?" he snarled to the squirrels who had gathered to watch the show. "Do you think I really wanted those grapes? Of course not. They are probably sour, anyway."

Fox left mumbling to his stomach, nose, eyes, mouth, and feet. "Quite likely those grapes weren't worth eating, anyway."

The squirrels, sitting in the branches, shook their heads. "You could have asked for a little help, Fox," they called. "We would have been happy to shake you down a bunch of grapes."

But it was too late. Besides, by now Fox was convinced that the grapes were sour.

Wind and the Sun

The day was brilliant. Sun was shining gloriously. Wind swirled leaves on the ground. Sun and Wind struck up a conversation. It was friendly enough, at first. They began talking about the weather, as most folks do when they meet. "Fine day," said Sun, proud of his golden head, shimmering on a blanket of blue sky.

"Indeed," agreed Wind, dancing amid the branches of trees. "Perfect," said Sun, "just a tingle of chill in the air. The way I like it."

"Yes! A little briskness is what people like," replied Wind.

"Actually, I think they prefer my warmth on their backs," replied Sun, a little perturbed.

"Not at all," answered Wind. "Too much sun makes people sweat. They feel better when it's cooler."

"I beg to differ," argued Sun, feeling bolder. "After all, how could wheat grow, be harvested, and ground into flour without me beating down nice and hot!"

"Well, if you are talking about importance," Wind responded with irritation, "it is I, who whips clouds full of rain, who really makes farmers happy."

"Are you suggesting that you are more powerful and important than I?" bellowed Sun, now quite angry. "Ridiculous."

"Perhaps we should have a small contest to see who is more powerful, you or me," said Wind, with a tinge of nastiness. "Look at that man there, walking down the road with the cloak upon his shoulders. Let us see who can remove it from him." With that Wind began to blow hard. The man, indeed, almost lost his cloak. In fact, it almost flew from his back, lifting him off his feet.

"There, you see?" said Wind, "I almost had the cloak off his back with just a little blow."

"Well, watch this!" said Sun. He beat golden rays upon the man's back. Just as the man was about to take off his cloak from the heat, the Wind unleased an icy blast, chilling the man to the bone. The man clasped the cloak about him like a shroud.

"Rats!" snarled Wind, as Sun beat down upon the man with more intensity. The man was so overcome with the heat he thrust the cloak from him, grasping for air. "I have won!" declared Sun, proudly.

"For the moment," replied Wind, making a hasty retreat.

"Such weather," said the man when he got home. "It has gone from hot to cold and back again." His wife looked outside. "Looks like rain," she said. Clouds had begun to form over the sky, blocking out the sun. "Why, it was brilliant a few minutes ago," said the man. "Not a cloud in the sky. Now it looks like rain. Such weather."

The Bare Bones of Friendship

Charlie and Harry were hiking on a fine day. When they came to a fork in the trail, Charley said, "Let's take the south fork."

Harry said, "I heard that bears were recently seen on that path. Let's take the north fork, it's safer."

"Nonsense," said Charley. "I talked with the ranger yesterday and he said nothing about bears. Let's take the south fork." So they did. They hadn't gone far when they heard a low growl.

"What's that noise?" whispered Harry.

"I didn't hear a thing," said Charley. "You are being jumpy for no reason. Let's go." But as soon as they had gone around a small bend in the path, they saw a bear coming toward them. Charley shoved Harry aside and climbed a nearby tree.

"Hey! Wait, Charley, wait for me." But Charley was already up the tree. "Don't climb up this tree, Harry. The branch won't hold two of us." The bear was coming closer and there was nothing for Harry to do but fall to the ground and play dead.

Harry lay there still, his heart pounding. The curious bear lumbered over and pawed him gently. But Harry didn't move. Charley clung to the branch of his tree, watching. No one moved or said a thing until the bear went away. Charley scrambled down from the tree and ran past Harry yelling, "Let's get out of here!" Charley didn't wait to see if Harry was behind him.

"Hey! Charley, wait for me," called Harry, charging after him. But Charley didn't even turn around. He just kept going. "With friends like you, Charley, who needs enemies!" called Harry. But Charley didn't hear him. He was too far ahead.

ANANSE THE SPIDER TALES—RETOLD BY LYNN RUBRIGHT

Why Spiders Hide in Ceiling Rafters

When Sky-god's mother died, many animals came to the funeral. Ananse wanted to sing the best grieving song, so he asked Jaybird,

Monkey, and Sheep—all fine singers—to go with him to the funeral. They were surprised when Ananse said, "I will carry you to the funeral in my sack, you will not even need to walk."

"But why?" they asked. "Never mind," said Ananse. "Besides not having to walk to the funeral, I will share Sky-god's feast with you."

Of course Jaybird, Monkey, and Sheep thought it was peculiar, but they agreed. When Ananse arrived at Sky-god's hut, he tugged on the sack, and from inside Jaybird, Monkey, and Sheep joined Ananse in a beautiful grieving song. Sky-god came out to listen.

Sky-god was impressed with Ananse's many voices and loud wailing. He ordered a special feast to honor Ananse's remarkable grieving song. Ananse savored every bite of the delicious food, sharing nothing with his friends.

Ananse's full belly made him drowsy. While he napped, the angry Jaybird, Monkey, and Sheep crept from the sack and hid in the bush, but not before filling the sack with stones.

The next day Sky-god summoned the elders to his hut to listen to Ananse's amazing funeral song. Ananse began to sing, tugging on the sack for his friends to join in, but no harmonies came forth. The elders laughed. "What is so special about Ananse's song?" they asked.

Sky-god said, "What happened to the many voices with which you sang yesterday?" Ananse sang louder. He danced about, pulling and yanking on the sack. But no voices joined his own.

Suddenly, Jaybird, Monkey, and Sheep jumped out from the brush, singing a beautiful funeral song of their own. Sky-god, enraged at the disrespectful trick Ananse had played on him, banished him from his presence. Ashamed, Ananse ran all the way home and hid in the ceiling rafters of his hut.

You can often find him there today.

How Wisdom Came into the World

Ananse was known for his tricks and his greed. He wanted the most of everything for himself: the most yams, the most corn, the biggest helping from the stew pot. When he found a large gourd that he heard contained all the wisdom in the world, he wanted to keep it for himself.

He decided to stash the gourd high in a tree for safe keeping. Tying the gourd in front of his belly with a cord, Ananse struggled to climb the tree. But he kept slipping and sliding back down the trunk.

One of Ananse's sons came by. "Hey! Papa, you would have better luck if you tied the gourd on your back." Ananse turned and scowled at his son. "Go away, what do you know!"

Ananse's son chuckled. "I can see that you are having trouble. Why not carry that gourd on your back?"

"I am the one who has all the wisdom in the world, not you. It is right here in this gourd." Ananse was much better at giving advice than taking it. Besides, he was irritated that his own son seemed to have some wisdom of his own.

Ananse looked so silly pushing the gourd up the tree with his belly that his son could not help laughing.

Suddenly, Ananse lost his grip and slid all the way down the tree trunk. The gourd slipped onto the ground and broke. Wisdom floated out, drifting everywhere on the wind.

"Quick," Ananse ordered his son, "help me gather the wisdom." But it was too late. Villagers came running, collecting what they could. Of course, they kept what they found to use in their own lives.

That is why to this day everyone in the world has a little wisdom, even Ananse; but no one has too much.

Ananse's Bargain

One growing season Ananse did not tend his crop of corn. When he did not water the tender plants, the hot African sun burned the leaves and young ears. He let weeds choke the slender stalks. At harvest time, there was very little corn. The crop had been nearly destroyed by his laziness.

But Ananse decided he would harvest what little grain there was and find a way to get a good price at market.

Since there was not much corn to sell, Ananse thought of a way to make it seem like the sack he carried to market was full of corn. "I fill the sack with pebbles, and cover only the top of the sack with corn," he said to himself, pleased with his cleverness.

Sweating, Ananse carried the sack to market in the hot sun. As he sat to rest, Ananse noticed a man coming down the road carrying a basket of yams. Ananse loved yams much more than corn. His mouth began to water. "Ho, friend, what fine yams you have there."

"Indeed," said the stranger, "I have worked all season cultivating my field of yams. See how fine they are." The stranger pulled a yam from his basket. It was very large and looked sweet and tender.

"Would you like to trade this fine sack of corn for that basket of yams?" asked Ananse, running his fingers through the corn on top of his sack.

The stranger said, "That is a fine idea. Then neither of us must travel all the way to market, and we both will have made a fine trade."

Ananse exchanged his corn for the stranger's yams. The basket of yams seemed very heavy, but Ananse didn't complain. His mouth watered at the thought of yams for supper. But when he got home, he found only a few yams on top of the basket. Furious at the trick that the stranger had played on him, he yelled for his wife.

"Aso! Come here and look. I have been cheated! Only the top of this basket is covered with yams, the rest of the basket is filled with rocks!" Ananse was furious at the trick the stranger had played on him. He was ready to find him and challenge him. But Aso said, "And what if he has discovered the trick you played on him with your sack of corn?" Ananse didn't want to be reminded of that.

Aso shook her head and chuckled at the tricks Ananse and the stranger had played on each other. "Each one deserves what he got," she thought. But whether she said it out loud, I do not know.

Ananse Visits Turtle

Just as Ananse was sitting down to a delicious dinner of fried yams, fufu, and spiced chicken, Turtle knocked at the door. It is a West African custom to always invite a guest to share your food, but Ananse, pretending not to hear, kept eating. "Brother Ananse, it's me, Turtle. Are you home?" The knocking grew louder.

Grumbling, Ananse answered the door. "Good evening, Turtle, you are just in time to share my dinner. But since you are dusty from your journey, please go wash your feet in the river first. It is not polite to enter someone's house with dirty feet."

Of course Turtle hurried to wash his feet. When he returned, he noticed that Ananse had already eaten half the spiced chicken. With his mouth full, Ananse said, "Brother Turtle, look at your feet, now they are muddy. Surely you can't enter my house with muddy feet."

"How clumsy of me, Ananse. I will go wash again." As Turtle trudged to the river, Ananse gobbled up the last of the fufu. By the time he returned, walking on the grass, Turtle saw that Ananse's fine dinner was all gone.

"I'm so sorry that you took so long," said Ananse. "You can see that I had to eat everything or else it would have spoiled in this heat. But there are a few crumbs left, and you are welcome to them. Next time be sure to come with clean feet so you can enter my house and enjoy my food with me." Poor Turtle trekked on home with an empty belly.

Not long after this Ananse went fishing. But the fish were not biting. Suddenly, Ananse looked down into the water. There was Turtle at his table eating a fine meal of fish stew.

"No wonder the fish aren't biting today. Turtle has caught them all and is eating them for dinner. Well, I will just pay him a little visit." Ananse called to him from where he stood on the bank.

Turtle looked up and waved for Ananse to come down. "Ho! Friend," gurgled Turtle, with his mouth full, "dive down. As you can see, you are in time for dinner. "

Ananse's mouth watered; his stomach grumbled. Over and over he dived, but he could not make his furry spider body stay under the water. "Hurry, Ananse, or you will be too late," called Turtle, his mouth full.

Ananse filled his pockets with stones. "Well, friend Turtle," said Ananse, floating down to Turtle's table, "here I am!"

"Oh, I am sorry," said Turtle, "but you know it is impolite to eat with your jacket on."

Of course Ananse could not be rude. But when he took off his jacket, he floated to the top of the water and had no choice but to go home hungry. Besides, Turtle had finished the stew himself.

If Turtle and Ananse happened to think of the old African proverb, "He who sows nettles does not reap roses," only Turtle was smiling that day.

Ananse's Three Tasks

Ananse and his wife, Aso, were talking one evening about how they would like to tell stories around the fire. "But Ananse, you know that Sky-god keeps all the stories in a golden box under his bed. Besides, many have tried to get them and failed." Ananse said, "Then maybe it is time for me to try."

The next day Ananse went on the journey to Sky-god's house. Sky-god was irritated that somebody else wanted his golden box of stories. "Not for sale!" he growled. Ananse said, "I wouldn't think of buying them. Money is not good enough payment for your stories. But perhaps I could earn them by doing difficult tasks. That would be worthy payment."

Sky-god thought. "If you can accomplish three tasks, each more difficult than the one before, you deserve the golden box of stories, Ananse."

Ananse agreed to do anything Sky-god required. "First task is to bring me a hive of bees in this calabash." Sky-god loved honey, and thought if he had a beehive nearby he could have all he wished to eat.

Ananse traveled until he found honey bees gathering pollen in a field of clover. He did a little dance in their midst, singing. "Yes they can, no they can't all fit into this calabash." Of course, the curious bees proved that they could fit into the calabash by flying inside. Ananse popped on a cork, delivering the bees to the Sky-god, who was pleased.

"The next task is more difficult," growled Sky-god. "Bring me the biggest, meanest leopard in the jungle." Ananse convinced a leopard to crawl into a sack by making him believe there was something wonderful inside. Sky-god was impressed when the leopard was delivered to him, but then he insisted that now Ananse bring him the longest snake in the jungle.

Ananse preyed on the snake's vanity, promising to measure his great length by tying him to a long bamboo pole. Ananse refused to untie the snake before carrying him on the pole to Sky-god for the completion of his third task.

Sky-god, true to his word, gave Ananse the golden box of stories. That night Ananse told a story to Aso as they sat around the fire.

To this day the Ashante people say that Ananse the spider is keeper of all the stories in the world. But, of course, now we know many of them, too, for as each story is told, it is also passed on, and on, and on.

Ananse's Dance

One day Ananse said to his wife, Aso, "Your mother is getting very old. It is hard for her to plant her rice. I will go help her today."

Aso was suspicious because Ananse rarely did anything nice for anyone without a reward, but she said, "Ananse, that would be a kind thing to do."

Ananse traveled to the clearing where his mother-in-law lived. He saw her bending close to the earth scattering rice seed. "Mother!" he called. "Let me sow the rice seed for you. Your back is breaking."

Ananse's mother-in-law was so grateful she said, "Ananse! You are kind. While you sow, I will simmer a pot of beans for supper." Of course, this is what Ananse really came for.

While Ananse sowed he also smelled the sweet beans simmering over an open fire. Suddenly, he found himself right next to the stew pot. When his mother-in-law was not looking, Ananse scooped up a hatful of bean stew. Just as he was taking a taste, his mother-in-law turned around. Ananse was embarrassed. He quickly put on his hat. But the bean stew was so hot on his head, Ananse began to jump and yell.

"Ananse! What is that fine new dance?" cried his mother-in-law.

"Oh, Mother, this is called the hat shaking dance," yelled Ananse, concealing his pain.

"I want to dance that dance, too. Dancing makes me feel young." Mother-in-law joined Ananse's dance. She made loud noises, just like Ananse's, thinking that he had composed a new song. But Ananse was shouting because the hot bean stew was burning his scalp. Soon neighbors came running to join in the dance and sing the new song.

But Ananse could no longer stand the pain. He pulled off his hat. Bean stew ran down his face. But worse, the hot stew had burned off all Ananse's hair. "Look! Ananse is bald," yelled the farmers, laughing.

Ananse was so embarrassed that he ran into the tall grasses near the river and hid among them for a long time. Finally, Ananse went home. Aso looked at his bald head, but she didn't ask what happened. She knew. Her mother had come to visit and told her what Ananse had done.

That is why today spiders have bald heads and like to hide in tall grasses.

Note: For more Ananse tales and other versions of these Ananse stories consult bibliography.

THE MAN WHO TRIED TO CHANGE HIS LUCK: A TRADITIONAL TALE, ADAPTED BY LYNN RUBRIGHT

Once there lived a man who had bad luck. When he tried to sell coffins, nobody died. When he tried to sell lanterns, the sun wouldn't set. It seems that he had no luck at all.

One day, in despair, he asked a wise neighbor for advice. "Why don't you journey to God and ask Him to change your luck?" So the man walked and walked until he came to a dark wood. There he met a hungry wolf who growled at him, licked his chops, and snarled, "I'm going to eat you!"

"Please don't eat me," pleaded the man. "I'm on my way to ask God to change my bad luck to good. If you have a request, I will ask God for you."

The wolf sneered. "I will let you go if you ask God why I eat twenty-four hours a day and am still hungry." The man agreed; the wolf let him go.

After a long walk, the man arrived at a quaint house with a charming garden. There stood a lovely maiden. "Where are you going?" she asked. "I'm on my way to ask God to change my luck," he answered.

"Would you please ask Him why I, who have everything, am still sad?" "Of course," said the man.

Traveling until exhausted, the man rested under a tree. The tree said, "Why are you so weary?" The man told him about his long journey to find God to ask Him to change his luck. "Ahhh!" said the tree. "Would you be so kind as to ask God why half my leaves are green and the other half are brown?" The man said he would be happy to ask.

Finally, the man found God resting at the foot of a great mountain. "Please, God," said the man, bowing low, "Would you please change my luck? Nothing I try works out for me. I fail at everything."

God said, "I promise you this. If you look for better luck, you will find it."

He thanked God and assured him that he would surely look for better luck. Before leaving, he relayed to God the questions of the tree, maiden, and wolf. And God gave him the answers.

On the way home the man looked for luck everywhere. Resting under the tree with the wilted leaves, the man told the tree, "By the way, God told me to tell you that buried treasure presses against your roots, keeping water from feeding your wilted branches."

As the man left to continue his search for luck, the tree cried after him, "Wait! Come dig up the treasure, it is yours!" "No I can't, I have to look for my luck."

When he approached the lovely maiden, the man said, "God has told me to tell you that when you marry and share your wealth, you will be happy."

"Wait," called the maiden, who fancied the kindly man. "Won't you stay for tea? Perhaps you can marry me!" "No, I can't, I have to look for my luck." Off he hurried down the road.

Finally, exhausted from his search for luck he rested in the forest. The wolf appeared. "Well! Has God changed your luck?"

"That's not the way He works," said the man wearily. "He said if I looked, I would find better luck myself. I have been looking, but so far no luck has come my way." Then he told the wolf about the maiden and the tree and God's messages for them.

"Hummmmmm!" mused the wolf. "And what did God tell me to do for my insatiable hunger?"

The man said, "He said to tell you that when you eat one foolish man, you will never be unduly hungry again."

The wolf threw back his head and laughed. "That will be easy," he said, and after a quick chase through the woods, the wolf caught the foolish man and swallowed him whole.

Appendix A
Then and Now
A Family Folklore Interdisciplinary Storytelling Unit

Adaptable for Grades One Through Eight

The family folklore storytelling unit can be planned to embrace language arts, social studies, math, science, music, and art—and the unit can span a week or a full semester.

LANGUAGE ARTS ACTIVITIES IN THE FAMILY FOLKLORE UNIT

- Collect adages passed down from previous generations that shape present family values. Write stories, essays, poetry using them.
- Extend multicultural literature on family themes through discussion, role play, creative drama, and puppetry.
- Interview family members and friends as resource material for story and play writing.
- Keep a journal on family traditions, trips, holidays, rituals.
- Write letters to family members to gather information about family traditions.
- Write, tell, and dramatize family stories.
- Make videos of family elders telling stories, anecdotes.
- Write poetry based on personal experiences.

SOCIAL STUDIES IN THE FAMILY UNIT

- Collect family sayings, slogans, mottoes, proverbs.
- Discuss family values as reflected in foods, recipes, remedies, etc.
- Discuss trades, professions, and work ethics of family members.

Study:

- Arts and crafts practiced by family members then and now
- Folklore, customs, literature of countries from which families emigrated
- Maps, geography, economies of native countries
- Research the following as they relate to your family history:

   changes in clothing styles
   laws and general values
   natural disasters (floods, earthquakes, tornadoes, and other natural disasters)
   technological changes
   transportation then and now
   wars and depressions

MATH AND SCIENCE

- Construct a detailed family tree.
- Graph genetic similarities and differences in your family.
- Make maps of places and communities where you've lived.
- Measure height, weight of family members.

ART

- Assemble collages or photograph albums that reflect favorite foods, activities, and memories of your family's past.
- Design, make a family folklore quilt.
- Build a diorama of family, town, farm scenes.
- Illustrate book of family stories.
- Prepare multimedia slide show on your family.
- Paint or photograph a family portrait.
- Make puppets to use in a family theme play.
- Write and illustrate a book of favorite recipes.

MUSIC

- Write a songbook of favorite family songs.
- Write, illustrate a chart or poster depicting musical instruments the family plays.
- Describe and demonstrate excerpts from favorite family dances, plays, or party games.

FESTIVAL OF FAMILY FOLKLORE: FINALE

A class or an all-school storytelling festival, displays of writing, presentations of research projects; arts and crafts demonstrations, plays, and puppet shows can all be part of the final event of the family folklore unit.

GETTING STARTED

Check signals with the school principal before starting the family folklore unit. Ask the principal to approve materials sent to parents.

A letter must go to parents explaining the purpose of the family unit: not to pry, but to help children discover and celebrate their cultural backgrounds through family stories, traditions, heirlooms, recipes, arts, and crafts. Some students may be from cultures where it might be thought an intrusion to share family information in school, so you must be sensitive to such possibilities.

Sample Letter to Parents

Dear Parents:

Our class will soon begin a study of *Then and Now*, a family folklore unit. We are fortunate to have in our class children from many cultural backgrounds. This study will give us an opportunity to reflect on, learn about, and celebrate our similarities and differences. It will also show us how growing up today is different from when our parents, grandparents, and older friends were young.

Our unit will include writing and researching of family stories that teach values and contain such things as adages, recipes, or folk remedies. We hope that old photographs, letters, and newspapers will be among resources for stories the children will develop. Parents, grandparents, and family friends will be invited to schedule classroom visits to share stories of their youth or folktales of a particular culture.

The enclosed questionnaire will help us determine how we might best use your help, should you choose to be part of our unit. Please ask your child to return the completed survey to me. Thank you for your comments and your possible participation.

Sincerely,

Questionnaire

Name _____

Relationship to student _____

Home phone _____

1. Would you be willing to come to class to share a family story or stories from your own childhood?
   _____ Yes
   _____ No
2. Do you have a special skill, such as quilting or woodworking, to share with the class?
   _____ Yes
   _____ No
   If Yes, what is your special skill? _____
3. Do you have any suggestions to help make our family folklore unit more meaningful for your child?

   _____

   _____

   _____

   _____

Please send this questionnaire back to school with your child as soon as possible. Thanks for your help!

As the unit develops, additional questionnaires can assist class members in the research necessary to enrich learning. During one family folklore unit, fifth-grade teachers Carol Sipes and Nancy Berg distributed the following research-oriented survey form.

Questionnaire for Student Use

Student Name _____ Date _____

You are a historian. Your purpose is to find or discover family stories, folklore, and traditions. Please interview a parent, grandparent, great-grandparent, or other older friend or adult relative. You can use your own words to make these questions more interesting. You can also make up your own questions.

Name of Person Interviewed_____

Male _____ Female _____ Age _____

1. Where were you born?_____

2. Where did you spend your early years?_____

   _____

   _____

3. How was going to school when you were young different from going to school today?

   _____

   _____

4. What was the main method of transportation when you were young?

   _____

   _____

5. Describe your childhood neighborhood.

   _____

   _____

6. Describe some games you played as a child.

   _____

   _____

7. What was your favorite toy?

   _____

   _____

8. What was your mother's favorite remedy for the common cold or flu?

   _____

   _____

9. What funny or embarrassing moment do you remember from your childhood?

   _____

   _____

   _____

   _____

10. Did you ever experience a war, or natural disaster, or an historical event?

_____

_____

11. How did you meet your husband or wife?

_____

_____

12. What do you remember about your grandparents?

_____

_____

13. What did you want to be when you grew up?

_____

_____

14. Do you think life is more or less difficult than when you were a child? Why?

_____

_____

Other questions could be asked about exciting or frightening moments, first dates, parties, family traditions, hardships, turning points, good and bad advice, or family sayings, adages, and admonitions.

Note: See Chapter 11, History Telling, for suggestions on gathering oral histories through the use of tape recorders. Another approach: use a video recorder to tape the interview.

Appendix B
Storytelling, Movement, and Drama Exercises

Our children's theater troupe, Metro Theater Circus, regularly played storytelling, movement, and drama games to release tensions, stretch imaginations, and sharpen interactive skills. Ideas that grew from our playful interaction became the foundation for our performances.

Regularly practiced during the school day, these kinds of activities increase creativity, develop concentration and listening skills, strengthen verbal and nonverbal communications, and expand the powers of imagination and inventive thinking.

MOVEMENT VOCABULARY

LEVELS	TEMPO	MOVEMENT	QUALITIES
high	fast	strong	weak
middle	slow	small	large
low		heavy	light
		fluid	rigid

WAYS TO MOVE

bending	leaping	soaring
contracting	marching	spreading
crawling	plopping	stomping
creeping	plunging	stretching
expanding	pulling	swaying
exploding	pushing	swirling
falling	shaking	tiptoeing
floating	shuffling	tripping
flying	skipping	turning
hopping	sliding	twirling
jumping	slithering	twisting

Some movements are done in place (nonlocomotor); some are done from here to there (locomotor): diagonally, sideways, backward, forward. Creating and repeating patterns, using different levels, tempos, and changing dynamics of intensity, results in expanded movement vocabularies that can enhance many of the following exercises.

STORYTELLING, MOVEMENT, DRAMA EXERCISES

One Minute Story (Grade 4 up)

Objectives:
To stimulate inventive thinking, increase ability to articulate ideas, focus on one topic at a time, and practice skills of improvisational speaking.

Process:

1. Objects are spread out on a large table or on the classroom floor (examples: blanket, Coke bottle, soda can, picnic basket, basketball, paint can—any objects will do).
2. Taking turns, students pick up an object and spontaneously make up and tell a one-minute story about it. Stories can be based on a child's life experiences or be totally invented on the spot. *Note:* As an alternative, the leader may ask players to take an object from a large paper bag in the front of the room, adding spontaneity to the exercise.

Secret Words (Grade 3 up)

Objectives:

To compose a round robin story; practice listening, concentration, inventive thinking skills and oral expression; and learn more about story structure.

Process:

1. Players work in small clusters.
2. Leader distributes two or three cards to each person. Each card contains one word, usually a noun (although cards can be mixed with adjectives and adverbs). Players keep the cards to themselves, not divulging contents.

3. One player voluntarily begins to tell a story, using the secret word in some way: "Once upon a time, a brown *bear* showed up in front of our candy store." (*Bear* was the secret word.) The story is then passed to other storytellers who insert their secret words, adding to the story.
4. Following the exercise, the story and secret words are discussed. Players brainstorm what could make the story more interesting or suspenseful. The story can then be acted out or written down.

Nonsense Language (Grade 4 up)

Objectives:

To practice self-expression and practice communicating with others using a made-up nonsense language (made-up words and syllables similar to gibberish).

Process:

1. Leader speaks a nonsense language to demonstrate how voice level, voice speed, and phrasing can convey the illusion that one is speaking a real language.
2. Working in pairs, players dialogue in nonsense language.
3. Audience members guess who the characters speaking a nonsense language might be, as well as the setting for the dialogue and topic being discussed.

Magic Bag (Grade 1 up)

Objectives:

To develop pantomime skills, stretch the imagination, and learn how to comprehend a story and its components.

Process:

1. Leader tells the class a story, then pantomimes an imaginary magic bag, telling class members that all objects from story are contained in the magic bag.
2. Players take turns pulling objects from story out of magic bag and pantomime them as a character from the story would use the object.

3. Other players guess what character is being pantomimed and what object is being used when and where in the story.
4. The object is returned to the magic bag and another person takes a turn.

Extension 1:

Another player enters the space as different character from the story and interacts with person #1, who is pantomiming an object in the space.

Extension 2:

1. Contents of the magic bag can relate not to a story but to a subject being studied, such as a historical event or current ecological, environmental, or social issue.
2. Players pull imaginary objects from the bag that relate to the agreed-upon topic, playing out characters and settings.
3. Audience members guess who is playing, where, when, and why.

Moving Characters (Grade 5 up)

Objectives:

To learn how movement influences the actions of characters in a story and to practice pantomime skills.

Process:

1. Players line up around perimeter of play space.
2. As the leader beats drum or plays music, players one by one move across the open space as pantomimed characters from the story they are studying.
3. Other players guess the identities of each pantomimed character.

Extension 1:

1. Players stand in a circle.
2. One person enters the circle and pantomimes a character from a specific story.

3. Other students enter the circle, pantomiming other characters from the story. Dialogue further develops the scene.

Extension 2:

1. Players stand in circle.
2. After agreeing upon a specific topic or theme, students move into the circle one by one, pantomiming characters appropriate to an agreed-upon theme. Players must know who they are, where, when, and why.
3. Nonverbally, they interact in pantomime.
4. Dialogue can be added when the pantomimed characters clearly demonstrate they know who and where they are, doing what and why.

Ball Game (Grade 5 up)

Objectives:

To develop skills of concentration by pantomiming an object using a sense of timing, rhythm, and weight.

Process:

1. Players stand in a circle, leader pantomimes throwing a baseball, for example, to someone on rim of circle.
2. A student catches the imaginary ball and throws it to someone else; that pantomimed motion continues as students receive and throw the ball.
3. During game, pantomime balls of a different texture, size, and weight (Ping-Pong balls, footballs, volleyballs) are thrown around the circle.

Pass It On! Creating Something from Nothing (Grade 1 up)

Objectives:

To hone pantomime skills, stretch the imagination, and stimulate creative and inventive thinking skills.

Process:

1. Players stand in a circle.
2. One player pantomimes an object such as a toothbrush, ice cream cone, or pair of roller blades.
3. That player, in pantomime, passes the object to the next player who transforms the passed object into another object, using the powers of imagination and creative thinking. This step of transforming pantomime objects is repeated all the way around the circle. *Note:* Leader encourages students to make each pantomimed object as real as possible by sensing its weight, texture, size, taste, smell.

Pass It On II (Grade 1 up)

Objectives:

To practice pantomime skills, stretch the imagination, develop powers of concentration and inventive thinking skills.

Process:

1. Standing in a circle, players take turns pantomiming objects from a wooden rod. Example: rod becomes tennis racket, comb, toothbrush.
2. Player using the rod as object passes it to the next player, who transforms the previous object (example: rod as toothbrush) into something else (toothbrush as comb). The exercise is repeated until everyone in the circle has participated.

Improvisational Group Pantomimes (Grade 5 up)

Objectives:

To experience imaginative and cooperative group play, to practice concentration and improvisational skills, and to foster an appreciation of the humor inherent in improvisational play.

Process:

1. Leader pantomimes using an object, such as a lawn mower.

2. One by one players enter the space and pantomime using other objects appropriate to the first player's pantomime object (lawn mower). Example: Player enters space and pantomimes raking the grass cuttings made from lawn mower into pile. Another player enters and pantomimes putting pile of grass cuttings into bag. *Note:* As players enter the game, they pantomime any activity that would take place in a garden. They can work individually or interact with other "gardeners" in pantomime.

Plate Dance (Grade 1 up)

Objectives:

To expand movement vocabulary.

Process:

1. Players put a paper plate under each foot.
2. To a steady drumbeat or recorded music, players slide/move around the play space with each foot on paper plate.
3. Leader may change the level, direction, or quality of movement through side coaching or altering the music, which may be classical, jazz, rock, country, etc.

Mummy Dance (Grade 1 up)

Objectives:

To become more aware of the range of bodily movements, to release inhibitions, and to nurture skills of concentration and listening.

Process:

1. Class members arrange themselves evenly in the play space.
2. Players imagine that they are tightly wrapped mummies, standing straight and completely bound.
3. To music or drum cue, mummies free themselves from the imaginary wraps—starting with fingers, hands, arms, then head, shoulders, torso, legs, and feet—until they are moving freely.

Exploring Space (Grade 1 up)

Objectives:

To further expand one's movement vocabulary by moving through space, leading with various body parts, changing levels, intensity, tempo, and direction of movement.

Process:

1. Players arrange themselves evenly in the play space.
2. Using music or drumbeat, leader cues players to move in all directions through the space favoring a body part, such as, for example, the nose, an elbow, a hip, or the head.
3. Leader coaches players to move in a variety of ways, not bumping each other (see movement chart).

From Here to There (Grade 3 up)

Objectives:

To further refine movement vocabularies.

Process:

1. Players line up around the play space perimeter.
2. Leader cues with music or drumbeat; one by one, players move diagonally across the space, demonstrating aspects of the movement vocabulary.

Space Walk (Grade 1 up)

Objectives:

To stretch the imagination and senses and further enhance movement vocabulary.

Process:

1. Players stand evenly in the play space.

2. Leader calls out substances (peanut butter, a dense forest, water, or jelly) that players will imagine they are moving through in pantomime.

Marionettes (Grade 5 up)

Objectives:

To expand the imagination and develop powers of concentration.

Process:

1. Pairs of players become puppeteers and marionettes.
2. Person playing puppeteer stands on a stool behind partner playing marionette.
3. The marionette moves as if imaginary strings are attached to its head, elbows, arms, wrists, hips, legs, and feet and are being manipulated by the puppeteer.
4. The puppeteer mirrors the marionette's movement.

Marionette Dance (Grade 5 up)

Objectives:

To further expand powers of imagination and concentration.

Process:

1. Pairs of marionettes face each other; puppeteer partners stand behind each marionette.
2. On musical cue, marionettes begin to dance.
3. Puppeteers again mirror the movements of their marionettes *as if puppeteers are initiating movement.*

Raggedy Ann and Raggedy Andy (Grades 1 through 3)

Objectives:

To use movement vocabularies to practice fluidity of dance movements.

Process:

1. Players imagine they are floppy stuffed Raggedy Ann and Andy dolls.
2. To drumbeat or music, players, as dolls, come to life and dance with loose and floppy movements.

Mirror Game (Grade 4 up)

Objectives:

To develop concentration, coordination, and cooperation skills.

Process:

1. Pairs of players work simultaneously during this exercise.
2. To drum or musical cues, partner *A* starts to move slowly; partner *B*, in close eye contact with *A*, reflects the movement so closely that one cannot tell who is leading.
3. Partners take turns leading the movement. *Note:* Partners can portray characters from stories as they reflect each other's movements.

Changing the Movement (Grade 3 up)

Objectives:

To hone skills of concentration and observation; to practice keeping tempo and rhythmic flow.

Process:

1. One person becomes "It."
2. Person who is "It" leaves the room briefly.
3. Another class member in the circle becomes the "It" who initiates a movement, such as snapping a finger or stomping a foot. Players in the circle immediately mirror "It's" movement, which constantly changes. Players mirror these movement changes.
4. The first "It" reenters the room, goes into the center of the circle and tries to guess who on the rim of circle is "changing the movement." When the "It" in mid-circle guesses correctly, a new round begins with a new "It" in the middle and a new "It" who changes the

action. *Note:* Player who is changing the movement can do a series of gestures that reflect qualities of characters in a story that has been told.

Collecting Movements (Grade 1 up)

Objectives:

To develop ability to recall movements in sequence, practice coordination, and develop a sense of tempo and rhythm.

Process:

1. Players arrange themselves in a circle.
2. One person starts the exercise by moving one body part rhythmically, such as an arm, to a four-beat count.
3. All players then repeat the movement.
4. The person to the right of the leader in the circle initiates another body movement.
5. As the exercise progresses, each person along the circle adds, in turn, another movement. All preceding movements are repeated in sequence before adding on the new movement.

Making Machines with Body Parts (Grade 4 up)

Objectives:

To refine skills of concentration and cooperation, to stimulate creative thinking, and to practice movement vocabulary.

Process:

1. Players sit on floor in front of an empty play space.
2. One player enters the space and assumes a pose, then repeatedly moves one body part, such as an arm.
3. A second player enters the space and begins to move in juxtaposition with the first player.
4. A third player enters the space with another body move that relates in some creative way to the first two players.
5. As more players enter the space and begin moving, the result should be the creation of a huge eclectic machine with many parts. *Note:* Sound can be added to each movement.

Extension 1: (Grade 5 up)

1. Pairs or small groups work together and decide what kind of machine to create: a lawn mower, wheelbarrow, or washing machine, for example.
2. Pairs or small groups of players create their machine as the class observes and guesses what machine the players are portraying.

Sculptures (Grade 5 up)

Objectives:

To develop improvisational and pantomime skills as well as to refine skills of concentration.

Process:

1. Players sit in a circle.
2. Leader spins one player in center of circle who turns around and freezes in an unusual or sculpture-like position.
3. Sculpture comes to life as character from a story players are currently studying—or historical figures, or persons currently in the news or well known in school or in the local community.
4. The class guesses who is being portrayed by the person in the circle, as well as something about that person: what he/she is doing, where the action is, and why. *Note:* The person playing the living sculpture can begin a monologue from the point of view of the character being portrayed. Others can enter the scene and add dialogue.

Appendix C
Book Making

The following instructions, designed by Marie Theerman, third-grade teacher, are for a book of accordion-folded panels that children can create themselves from sheets of 12" by 18" good quality drawing paper.

MATERIALS

Three 12" by 18" sheets of white (or other color) good quality paper. Optional: one sheet 9" by 12" tag board cut in half lengthwise creating two 4½" by 12" pieces for front and back book cover panels. These panels can be illustrated and laminated before gluing onto front and back of book for added durability.

DIRECTIONS

Fold each of three sheets of drawing paper into four sections measuring 12" by 4½".

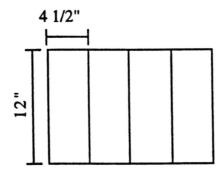

Overlap and glue one section of each sheet, making ten panels.

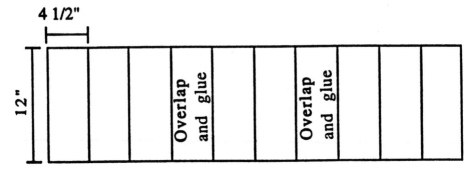

Fold all ten panels accordion style.

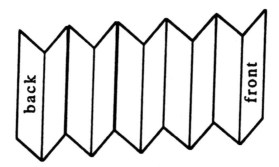

The front panel is the book cover, to be illustrated with title and author.

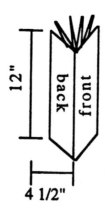

Possibilities for illustrating story text on the interior panels include:

One long mural-like illustration that flows from panel to panel interspersed with text.
Illustrations and text on each panel.
Pop-up illustrations of construction paper.

Pockets added for inserting special kinds of writing to illuminate text: letters, directions, secret messages, codes, or paperdoll types of removable characters.

Glossary

Storytelling and related arts may be exciting, liberating, and motivational, but mastery calls for concentration, determination, and discipline. The following terms are used throughout this book.

Auditory Cues

Start-stop signals the leader makes to begin and end an activity. A drumbeat, bell, or verbal cue begins or ends the action. A visual cue can also be used to start and stop action.

Group Structures

The exercises in this book use many *group structures:* individual, pairs, triads, quartets; large and small groups and circles. Leaders structure different-size groups to help students interact in different ways as they do exercises.

Locomotor and Nonlocomotor Movement

Locomotor refers to movement that is done "from there to there" moving through space; *nonlocomotor* refers to movement done in one's own work/play space.

Movement Vocabulary

Awareness of how body movement can express levels (high, low, middle), intensity (strong and weak), tempo (fast, slow), fluidity (soft, flowing), rigidity (sharp, angular), dimension (size), direction, locomotor (movement in place), nonlocomotor (movement here to there).

Notes

Suggestions and comments made by the leader after an exercise is complete. *Notes* include comments on how well the exercise worked;

whether the objective was met; how peers interacted to solve problems. Notes should accentuate what went well and include suggestions for what needs further development. Notes can be used for informal evaluation.

Participatory Storytelling

The storyteller invites the audience to "join in" the telling of the story being told by singing, repeating phrases, or contributing information at the request of the storyteller. The storyteller retains control of the story.

Personal Work/Play Space

Before a storytelling, music, movement, or drama activity begins, space needed for the activity is defined. Students create a *personal work/play space* by spreading arms, slowly turning in a circle defining a work/play space. Students do not invade another's space unless appropriate to the exercise. Sometimes the work/play space is a larger "stage" area where group work takes place.

Sensory Stretches

Exercises that develop the imagination and broaden awareness of and sensitivity to things seen, felt, tasted, smelled, heard.

Side Coaching

Suggestions from the leader to help students working on music, movement, drama, or story exercises refine their work, deepen understanding, or help move the action forward to completion. When a leader *side-coaches,* an auditory cue is often given by calling "freeze," beating a drum, or whispering directions to the players to further the action.

Simultaneous Exercises

When music, movement, drama and story exercises, are done by all the children, working individually, but simultaneously, in their work/play space.

Stage Space

Classroom desks are moved to predetermined space in room to create a "stage" area in the room. (May be a rug in the reading corner, a wide space in front of the blackboard, a circular space for "theater in the round" in center of room.) There should be floor room for an audience of students to observe their peers present individual and ensemble pieces.

Story Bones

Component parts of plot that make up stories:

- *setting:* where story takes place
- *characters:* who is in the story
- *incidents:* what are the things that happen in the story
- *conflict:* when and where there is tension, an argument, a fight between characters
- *crisis:* what is the most serious problem in the story
- *resolution:* how the story ends

Story Weaver

Person playing *story weaver* is in charge of a story-building exercise during which storyteller and audience create a story together improvisationally. This person can be an adult or student; the role may change during a story-weaving exercise.

Story Weaving

An improvisational story-building exercise out of which an original story evolves. The story weaver and audience work collaboratively to create the story; the story weaver weaves into the story what the audience adds to the story.

Work/Play Space

Space designated where students work on exercises. This space can be large or small depending on need.

Bibliography

CHAPTER ONE: BEYOND THE BEANSTALK

Bettelheim, Bruno. 1976. *The Uses of Enchantment: The Meaning and Importance of Fairy Tales*. New York: Alfred A. Knopf.

Chase, Richard. 1971. *The Jack Tales*. New York: Houghton Mifflin Company.

Davis, Donald. 1992. *Jack Always Seeks His Fortune: Authentic Appalachian Jack Tales*. Little Rock, AK: August House Publishers, Inc.

Haley, Gail E. 1988. *Jack and the Fire Dragon*. New York: Crown Publishers, Inc.

Jacobs, Joseph. 1967. *English Fairy Tales*. New York: Dover.

Opie, Peter and Iona. 1980. *The Classic Fairy Tales*. London: Granada Publishing, Ltd.

Ringgold, Faith. 1992. *Tar Beach*. New York: Crown Publishers.

———. 1993. *Dinner at Aunt Connie's House*. New York: Hyperion Books for Children.

CHAPTER TWO: FROG AND TOAD'S GARDEN

Gallimard, Jeunesse, and P. de Bourgoing; C. Broutin, illustrator. 1989. *The Tree: A First Discovery Book*. New York: Cartwheel Books, Scholastic, Inc.

Gallimard, Jeunesse, C. Delafosse, and Rene Metten. 1991. *Flowers: A First Discovery Book*. New York: Cartwheel Books (Scholastic).

Graves, Donald, and J. Hansen. 1983. "The Author's Chair." *Language Arts* 60: 176–183.

Heller, Ruth. 1983. *The Reason for a Flower*. New York: Scholastic, Inc.

Ingoglia, Gina. 1987. *Look Inside a Tree: A Poke and Look Learning Book*. New York: Grosset & Dunlap, Inc.

Jaspersohn, William; C. Eckart, illustrator. 1980. *How the Forest Grew*. New York: Greenwillow Books.

Krauss, Ruth; C. Johnson, illustrator. 1945. *The Carrot Seed*. New York: Scholastic, Inc.

Levy, Constance. 1991. *I'm Going to Pet a Worm Today and Other Poems*. New York: Margaret K. McElderry Books.

———. 1994. *A Tree Place and Other Poems*. New York: Margaret K. McElderry Books.

Lobel, Arnold. 1972. *Frog and Toad Together*. "The Garden." New York: Harper and Row.

———. 1984. *The Rose in My Garden*. New York: Scholastic, Inc.

Merrill, Claire; S. Swan, illustrator. 1973. *A Seed Is a Promise.* New York: Scholastic, Inc.

Moffett, James, and Betty Jane Wagner. 1992. *Student-Centered Language Arts, K–12.* Fourth Edition. Portsmouth, NH: Heinemann Educational Books. 26–30.

Romanova, Natalia; G. Spirin, illustrator. 1983. *Once There Was a Tree.* New York: Dial Books.

Ryder, Joanne and Lynne Chery. 1982. *The Snail's Spell.* New York: Scholastic, Inc.

CHAPTER THREE: *ROSIE'S WALK*

Interdisciplinary Farm Unit

Boyston, Angela. 1980. *Farm Animal Stories: The Hen.* New York: Warwick Press.

Chase, Edith. 1984. *The New Baby Calf.* New York: Scholastic. (illustrated by photographing pictures of clay).

DePaola, Tomie. 1973. *Charlie Needs a Cloak.* Englewood Cliffs, NJ: Prentice-Hall.

Duvoisin, Roger. 1987. *Petunia, the Silly Goose Stories.* New York: Knopf.

Ehlert, Lois. 1988. *Planting a Rainbow.* New York: Harcourt Brace Jovanovich.

———. 1990. *Color Farm.* New York: J. B. Lippincott.

Freedman, Russell. 1981. *Farm Babies.* New York: Holiday House. (excellent for cycles of life).

Heller, Ruth. 1981. *Chickens Aren't the Only Ones.* New York: Scholastic.

Hutchins, Pat. 1963. *Rosie's Walk.* New York: Macmillan.

Kraus, Ruth. 1945. *The Carrot Seed.* New York: Scholastic.

Nolan, Dennis. 1987. *The Joy of Chickens.* Englewood Cliffs, NJ: Prentice-Hall.

Patent, Dorothy H. 1984. *Farm Animals.* New York: Holiday House. (content rich).

Pinkney, Gloria and Jerry Pinkney. 1992. *Back Home.* New York: Dial Books.

Science Resources

"Incubating Eggs of Domestic Birds." Circular 530, July 1974. Clemson University cooperating with United States Department of Agriculture, Clemson, SC 29631.

"Incubation & Embryology. A Missouri Science Project Program Guide." University of Missouri Extension Division and the Missouri Department of Elementary and Secondary Education. P.O. Box 480, Jefferson City, MO 65101.

Video Resources

"Chick, Chick, Chick." Available in video format from Churchill Media, 12210 Nebraska Avenue, Los Angeles, CA 90025. (800) 334-7830.

"Pigs." Available in video format from Churchill Media, 12210 Nebraska Avenue, Los Angeles, CA 90025. (800) 334-7830.

"Rosie's Walk" (animated video). Weston Woods, Weston, CT 06880.
"Rosie's Walk" (Lynn Rubright tells story and children dramatize through movement; video format). Kaw Valley Films, Box 3900, Shawnee, KS 66203. (913) 631-3040.

CHAPTER FOUR: BELLEROPHON AND PEGASUS

D'Aulaire, Edgar and Ingri. 1962. *Book of Greek Myths.* Garden City, NY: Doubleday.
Graves, Donald. 1983. *Writing: Teachers and Children at Work.* Portsmouth, NH: Heinemann.
Russell, William. 1989. *Classic Myths to Read Aloud.* New York: Crown Publishers.

CHAPTER FIVE: THE SEA

Reeves, James. [1957] 1994. "Grim and Gloomy." *The Wandering Moon.* Oxford: Heinemann.
Spolin, Viola. 1983. *Improvisation for the Theater.* Evanston, IL: Northwestern University Press.

CHAPTER SIX: STORYTELLING AND MUSIC

Frazee, Jane, with Kent Kreuter. 1987. *Discovering ORFF: A Curriculum for Music Teachers.* New York: Schott.
Lobel, Arnold. 1980. *Fables.* "The Camel Dances." New York: Harper & Row.

Addresses

Executive Secretary
American Orff-Schulwerk Association
P.O. Box 391089
Cleveland, OH 44139-1089
(216) 543-5366
(for information on Orff chapters and workshops nationwide)

Australia National Council of Orff-Schulwerk Associations
P.O. Box 225
Strathfield 2135,
New South Wales, Australia
(02) 759-6796

MMB Music, Inc.
Contemporary Arts Building
3526 Washington Avenue
St. Louis, MO 63103

(314) 531-9635
(800) 543-3771

(a full line of Orff instruments available from MMB Music is listed in the Studio 49 Catalog; MMB Music Creative Arts Therapy and General Music Education Catalog lists other books and materials based on the Orff approach)

CHAPTER SEVEN: CHILDREN AS PLAYMAKERS AND PLAYWRIGHTS

Freeman, William, Placido A. Hoernicke, et al. 1994. *Access to the Arts: Education Curricula Modules in Art, Music, Drama, and Dance/ Movement for the Integration of the Arts in the Inclusive Classroom.* (Curriculum, Developmental Guideline in the Arts and Arts Training video). Kansas City, KS: Accessible Arts, Inc., 1100 State Avenue, Kansas City, KS 66102. (913) 281-1133.

Kent, Corita, and Jan Steward. 1992. *Learning by Heart: Teaching to Free the Creative Spirit.* New York: Bantam Books.

Mettler, Barbara. 1979. *Materials of Dance: Creative Art Activity.* Tuscson, AZ: Mettler Studios.

Rosenberg, Helene. 1987. *Creative Drama and Imagination: Transforming Ideas into Action.* New York: Holt, Rinehart and Winston.

Sark. 1991. *A Creative Companion: How to Free Your Creative Spirit.* Berkeley, CA: Celestial Arts.

CHAPTER EIGHT: LEARNING TALES TO TELL—QUICK AND EASY

Bauer, Caroline Feller. 1977. *Handbook for Storytellers.* Chicago: American Library Association.

Chase, Richard. 1976. *Grandfather Tales.* "Wicked John and the Devil," pp. 29–39. Boston: Houghton Mifflin Co.

Cooper, Pamela, and Rives Collins. 1992. *Look What Happened to Frog: Storytelling in Education.* Scottsdale, AZ: Gorsuch Scarisbrick Publishers.

DeSpain, Pleasant. 1993. *Thirty-Three Multi-Cultural Tales to Tell.* Little Rock, AK: August House Publishers, Inc.

Hamilton, Martha, and Mitch Weiss. *Children Tell Stories: A Teaching Guide.* Katonah, NY: Richard C. Owen Publishers.

Harrison, Annette. 1992. *Easy-to-Tell Stories for Young Children.* Jonesborough, TN: National Storytelling Press.

Livo, Norma, and Sandra A. Ritz. 1986. *Storytelling Process and Practice.* Littleton, CO: Libraries Unlimited.

McKissack, Patricia, and Ruthilde Kronberg. 1990. *A Piece of the Wind and Other Stories to Tell.* New York: Harper and Row.

Stevenson-Hobbs, Anne, ed. 1986. *Fables.* London: Victoria and Albert Museum.

Sutcliff, Rosemary. 1961. *Dragon Slayer: The Story of Beowulf.* New York: Puffin Books.

CHAPTER NINE: ANANSE THE SPIDER

Appiah, Peggy. 1967. *Tales of an Ashanti Father.* Boston: Beacon Press.

Arkhurst, Joyce C. 1964. *The Adventures of Spider.* New York: Scholastic.

————. 1972. *More Adventures of Spider.* New York. Scholastic Tales.

Bleeker, Sonia. 1966. *The Ashanti of Ghana.* New York: William Morrow.

Bosma, Betty. 1987. *Fairy Tales, Fables, Legends, and Myths: Using Folk Literature in Your Classroom.* New York: Teachers College Press.

Courlander, Harold. 1957. *Hat Shaking Dance, and Other Ashanti Tales from Ghana.* New York: Harcourt Brace Jovanovich.

Goodman, Jesse, and Kate Melcher. December, 1984. "Culture at a distance: An anthroliterary approach to cross-cultural education." *Journal of Reading,* 200–207.

Haley, Gail E. 1970. *A Story A Story.* New York: Atheneum.

McDermott, Gerald. 1972. *Anansi the Spider: A Tale from the Ashanti.* New York: Holt Rinehart and Winston.

Pelton, Robert. 1980. *The Trickster in West Africa: A Study of Mythic Irony and Sacred Delight.* Los Angeles: University of California Press.

Price, Christine. 1973. *Talking Drums of Africa.* New York: Charles Scribner's Sons.

Rachelson, Stan, and Grace Copeland. Spring 1983. "Webbing: A humanistic approach to curriculum development." *Journal of Humanistic Education* 7, 6–8.

Rattray, Robert. 1969. *Akan-Ashanti Folktales.* London: Oxford University Press.

Sherlock, Phillip M. 1954. *Anansi the Spider.* New York: Thomas Y. Crowell and Co.

CHAPTER TEN: FAMILY FOLKLORE

Ada, A. F.; K. Thompson, illustrator. 1993. *My Name Is Maria Isabel.* New York: Atheneum.

Adler, David; S. Byrd, illustrator. 1993. *A Picture Book of Anne Frank.* New York: Holiday.

Coerr, Eleanor; Bruce Degen, illustrator. 1989. *Josefina Story Quilt.* New York: Harper Collins Children's Books.

Flournoy, Valerie. 1985. *The Patchwork Quilt.* New York: Dial Books.

George, Jean Craighead. 1977. *My Side of the Mountain.* New York: Dutton.

Griffity, Helen; James Stevenson, illustrator. 1990. *Georgia Music.* New York: William Morrow.

Howard, Elizabeth F. 1991. *Aunt Flossie's Hats (And Crab Cakes Later).* New York: Clarion Books.

Johnston, Toni. 1985. *The Quilt Story.* New York: Scholastic.

————. 1988. *Yonder.* New York: Dial Books for Young Children.

Jordan, June. 1981. *Kimako's Story.* New York: Houghton Mifflin.

Kendall, Russ. 1992. *Eskimo Boy.* New York: Scholastic.

Levinson, Riki; Diane Goode, illustrator. 1985. *Watch the Stars Come Out.* New York: Dutton Children's Books.

Martin, Bill. 1966. *Knots on a Counting Rope.* New York: Holt, Rinehart, Winston.

McKissack, Patricia; Jerry Pinkney, illustrator. 1988. *Mirandy and Brother Wind.* New York: Alfred A. Knopf.

Murphy, Jim. 1993. *Across America on an Emigrant Train.* New York: Clarion Books.

Noble, Trina. 1988. *Apple Tree Christmas.* New York: Dial Books for Young People.

Ringgold, Faith. 1991. *Tar Beach.* New York: Crown.

Rylant, Cynthia. 1992. *Missing May.* New York: Orchard Books.

——— . 1985. *The Relatives Came.* New York: Bradbury Press.

Silverstein, Shel. 1981. "Little Abigail and the Beautiful Pony." *A Light in the Attic.* New York: Harper and Row, 120–121.

Stevenson, James. 1986. *When I Was Nine.* New York: Greenwillow Books.

Tate, Eleanora; E. Velasquez, illustrator. 1992. *Front Porch Stories at the One-Room School.* New York: Bantam Skylark.

Taylor, Mildred. 1976. *Roll of Thunder, Hear My Cry.* New York: Dial Press.

Turner, Ann; Ronald Himler, illustrator. 1985. *Dakota Dugout.* New York: Macmillan Children's Book Group.

Uchida, Yoshiko. 1971. *The Invisible Thread.* New York: Creative Arts.

Wilder, Laura. 1941. *Little House Books* (Series). New York: Harper Trophy Books.

——— . 1944. *Farmer Boy.* New York: HarperCollins.

Williams, David; W. Sandowski, illustrator. 1993. *Grandma Essie's Covered Wagon.* New York: Knopf.

CHAPTER ELEVEN: HISTORY TELLING

Graves, Donald, and J. Hansen. 1983. "The Author's Chair." *Language Arts* 60:176–183.

Moffett, James, and Betty Jane Wagner. 1992. *Student Centered Language Arts, K–12.* Portsmouth, NH: Boynton/Cook Publishers, Heinemann.

National Writing Project (NWP), an outgrowth of the University of California at Berkeley Bay Area Writers Project, was developed to help teachers become better writers. Since 1973 almost a million teachers, administrators, parents, and writers have participated in the programs sponsored by NWP at the 165 national and international training sites. For information write: National Writing Project, School of Education, 5627 Tolman Hall, University of California, Berkeley, CA 54720. (510) 647-0963.

Rachelson, Stan, and Grace Copeland. Spring 1983. "Webbing: A humanistic approach to curriculum development." *Journal of Humanistic Education.* 7.

CHAPTER TWELVE: ELDERTEL

Bunting, Eve. 1990. *How Many Days to America: A Thanksgiving Story.* New York: Clarion.

Clifford, E. 1985. *The Remembering Box.* New York: Houghton Mifflin.

Fox, Mem, Julie Vivas, illustrator. 1989. *Wilfred Gordon McDonald Partridge.* New York: Kane/Miller.

Greenfield, Eloise. 1988. *Grandpa's Face.* New York: Putnam/Philomel.

———. 1987. *Sister.* New York: Harper & Row.

Hoffman, Mary. 1991. *Amazing Grace.* New York: Dial Books for Young Readers.

MacLachlan, Patricia. 1980. *Through Grandpa's Eyes.* New York: HarperCollins.

Mathis, Sharon. 1975. *The 100 Penny Box.* New York: Viking Press.

Rylant, Cynthia. 1982. *When I Was Young in the Mountains.* New York: E. P. Dutton.

Stanley, Derry. 1992. *Children of the Dust Bowl: The True Story of the School at Weedpatch Camp.* New York: Crown.

CHAPTER THIRTEEN: STORYTELLING AND THE WRITING-READING PROCESS

Sources for Teaching Writing

Atwell, Nancy. 1987. *In the Middle: Writing, Reading, and Learning with Adolescents.* Portsmouth, NH: Boynton/Cook.

Berthoof, A. 1984. *Reclaiming the Imagination: Philosophical Perspective for Writers and Teachers of Writing.* Portsmouth, NH: Boynton/Cook.

Calkins, L. M. 1986. *The Art of Teaching Writing.* Portsmouth, NH: Heinemann.

Gardner, Howard. 1985. *Frames of Mind: The Theory of Multiple Intelligences.* New York: Basic Books, Inc.

Graves, Donald. 1983. *Writing: Teachers and Children at Work.* Portsmouth, NH: Heinemann.

Harste, Jerome, and Kathy C. Short, with Carolyn Burke. 1988. *Creating Classrooms for Authors: The Reading-Writing Connection.* Portsmouth, NH: Heinemann.

Moffett, James, and Betty Jane Wagner. 1992. *Student-Centered Language Arts, K–12.* Fourth Edition. Portsmouth, NH: Boynton/Cook Publishers, Inc.

CHAPTER FOURTEEN: ARTIST-IN-RESIDENCE PROGRAMS

Resources

Arts in Education Resources
Council for Basic Education
1319 F Street NW, Suite 900
Washington, DC 20004-1152
(202) 347-4171

(Offers fellowships for classroom teachers, and arts specialists for innovative independent four- to six-week summer institutes.)

Kennedy Center Alliance for Arts Education Network
Kennedy Center
Washington, DC 20566
(202) 416-8845
(Publication: Schools, Communities, and the Arts: A Research Compendium)

National Assembly of State Arts Agencies
1010 Vermont Avenue NW
Washington, DC 20005
(202) 347-6352

(Information on all state arts councils and six jurisdictions under the United States government that have arts councils offering artist-in-residence programs: District of Columbia, Northern Marianas, American Samoa, Guam, Puerto Rico, US Virgin Islands)

National Endowment for the Arts
Education and Access
1100 Pennsylvania Avenue NW
Washington, DC 20506
(202) 682-5438

National Gallery of Art
Education Division
4th Street and Constitution Avenue
Washington, DC 20565
(202) 737-4215

(Catalog of programs available to borrow by mail—slides, videos, teaching packets, videodiscs—and a directory of special programs available at art museums nationally)

Opera America
1156 15th NW Suite 810
Washington, DC 20005-1704
(202) 293-4466

(Opera America's *Music! Words! Opera!* series contains curricular materials—teacher guides and tapes—designed by master teachers and opera professionals for classroom teachers and music specialists. "Listen and Discover" introduces children to stories of opera. "Create and Produce" helps them write their own stories, setting them to music.)

Smithsonian Institution
Office of Elementary and Secondary Education (OESE)
Arts and Industries Building, Suite 1163
Washington, DC 20560
(202) 357-2404

(*Smithsonian Resource Guide for Teachers 1993–94* contains mostly free or inexpensive materials and lesson plans to enrich the classroom using interdisciplinary suggestions and lesson plans.)

Young Audiences
115 East 92nd Street
New York, NY 10128
(212) 831-8110

(A Network of Young Audience chapters provides educational programs and services to schools and cultural organizations nationwide.)

APPENDIX A: THEN AND NOW

Alessi, Jean, and Jan Miller. 1987. *Once upon a Memory: Your Family Tales and Treasures*. White Hall, VA: Betterway Publications, Inc.

Daniel, Lois. 1985. *How to Write Your Own Life Story: A Step by Step Guide for the Non-Professional Writer*. Chicago: Chicago Review Press.

Davis, Donald. 1993. *Telling Your Own Stories*. August House.

Gould, June. 1989. *The Writer in All of Us: Improving Your Writing Through Childhood Memories*. New York: E. P. Dutton.

Rosenbluth, Vera. 1990. *Keeping Family Stories Alive: A Creative Guide to Tapping Your Family and Love*. Point Roberts, WA: Hartley & Marks, Inc.

Rylant, Cynthia. 1982. *When I Was Young in the Mountains*. New York: E. P. Dutton.

Weitzman, David. 1975. *The Brown Paper School Presents My Backyard History Book*. Boston: Little, Brown and Company.

Welty, Eudora. 1984. *One Writer's Beginnings*. Cambridge, MA: Harvard University Press.

Zeitlin, Steven J., Amy J. Kotkin, and Holly Cutting Baker. 1982. *Celebration of American Family Folklore: Tales and Traditions from the Smithsonian Collection*. New York: Pantheon Books.

Zimmerman, William. 1982. *How to Tape Instant Oral Biographies*. New York: Guarionex Press, Ltd.

APPENDIX B: STORYTELLING, MOVEMENT, AND DRAMA EXERCISES

Barton, Bob, and David Booth. 1990. *Stories in the Classroom: Storytelling, Reading Aloud, and Role Playing with Children*. Portsmouth, NH: Heinemann.

Cooper, Pamela J., and Rives Collins. 1992. *Look What Happened to Frog*. Scottsdale, AZ: Gorsuch Scarisbrick, Publishers.

Peck, Judith. 1979. *Leap to the Sun: Learning Through Dramatic Play*, Englewood Cliffs, NJ: Prentice-Hall, Inc.

Scher, Anna, and Charles Verrall. 1985. *100 Plus Ideas for Drama*. Portsmouth, NH: Heinemann.

————. 1987. *Another 100 Plus Ideas for Drama.* Portsmouth, NH: Heinemann.

Spolin, Viola. 1983. *Improvisation for the Theater.* Evanston, IL: Northwestern University Press.

Stewig, John Warren. 1983. *Informal Drama in the Elementary Language Arts Program.* New York: Teachers College.

Stewig, John Warren, and Carol Buege. 1994. *Dramatizing Literature in Whole Language Classrooms.* New York: Teachers College.